Praise for *Overliked*

"*Overliked* by Rob Singleton is a tome for such a time as this. It's so easy to get our self-esteem and self-worth tied to likes and numbers. Through Pastor Rob's book, we learn how frivolous and fake it can all be and ultimately, how it can lead to a miserable and unfulfilled life if left unchecked. The tools, scriptures, and takeaways that Pastor Rob provides gently guide us to live a more authentic life. *Overliked* shows us that when we pretend to be perfect, the only person we are hurting is ourselves. But we find that our weaknesses become our strengths to help us touch, encourage, and heal others, not just impress them. Thank you for this very needed and essential book that helps us realize that being real is the only way to have a true connection with our Lord and our friends and family. This book is an important message for developing authenticity in our lives, which is far more critical than adding strangers, getting fake followers, and creating a heavily filtered life experience. I promise you will really 'LIKE' it."

—Kym Douglas, television personality, lifestyle expert, and author

"*Relevant Communicator—Contemporary Prophet—Radical Evangelist—* These are three apt descriptions that come to mind when I think about my good friend Rob Singleton whom I have known over the last twenty-five years beginning while we were doing Young Life in Dallas during our seminary days. Like a cultural surgeon, Rob exposes and examines the counterfeit culture of contemporary technology, which reveals that our hearts and souls are at risk. The very technology that we love so much and is attached to everything we do, cannot and does not deliver on its promises. It leaves all of us empty and desirous of more. Without condemning the technology, *Overliked* will help you navigate a new way forward that anchors the soul in genuine and lasting relationships—the kind of relationship that is only found in Jesus. Thank you, Rob, for rewiring and rebooting our heart to what truly matters and what truly lasts!"

—Ernie Frey, pastor and disciple-making missionary in Africa

"There is no man I respect more than Rob Singleton. When I was at the lowest and darkest point of my life, He was the truest friend, most available mentor, and the most epic prayer warrior. I think God had Rob on assignment to help open my eyes and bring me back. He reminded me that people need to return to being true, sacrificial, authentic friends and family and stop putting so much emphasis on being people pleasers. And I imagine, Rob is now on assignment for you. What you'll find in the pages of this book will be life lessons and transformative wisdom that will stick with you for a lifetime."

—Art TerKeurst, Chick-fil-A owner/operator

"Pastor Rob Singleton dares to dive deep into a painful addiction many in our culture drift into . . . getting trapped by the optics. It starts with social media 'likes' and runs rampant though our lives if we don't address it. As a widow, I have often stood apart from the crowd. How grateful I was for Pastor Rob's example. My four boys witnessed firsthand Pastor Rob's integrity through the tough experiences he talks about in this book. Let him lead you, as he often leads us. This fresh look at Scripture guides you out of fear of what others think and into the light of God's Truth. A must-read for finding God-centered fulfillment in an optics-driven world."

—Kitty Hinkle, founder of A Widow's Might Christian ministry

"Rob and I met in the early 2000s when social media was somewhat of a new and untested phenomenon. Podcasts were just becoming a thing. Church planters were popping up everywhere. And the sudden rise of platforms like Facebook and Twitter were making celebrities out of Christian leaders. But I got to know personally Rob and his heart for people as I spent time preaching for him at his church, and also eating meals around the table in his home with his family. Rob loves the Bible, and Rob loves the gospel—and that is why I trust him as a friend and brother. What he brings to us in this book is experience: decades of ministry, of pastoral care, of wisdom won in the trenches. Rob points out the deficiencies and dangers in living life virtually and the need we all have for true friendships with actual people, to know and be known by God and others. You will like *Overliked*, but more importantly, your soul will connect with the message in these pages."

—**Clayton King,** author of *Reborn* and *Stronger,* teaching pastor at Newspring Church, founder of Crossroads Camps and Conferences

"Wow! Talk about hitting you right between the eyes. *Overliked* spoke directly to me. I could see myself in the pages and stories that Pastor Rob shares. How many times have I gone back to the pictures I've posted for a like count update and to see what people had to say? *Overliked* drives home how our society has turned to social media platforms for the attention we so desire from one another and just how ineffective social media is to have true, deep, and meaningful relationships. It also speaks to how we need the one true relationship with God."

—**Travis Jones,** Dream Team Leader at The Summit Church

"I lived most of my life seeking approval from the world through money and status, until the only people who liked me were people money could buy. I was on a road straight to hell, fighting addiction and living in chaos, until four years ago when Jesus rescued me. He cast out my fear of never being enough. Pastor Rob Singleton shows us in this book how 'likes' from the world can't compare to the true love of Jesus Christ."

—Jason McCool, founder and chairman of
Executive Coating and Contracting

"Pastor Rob is a true example of how to live full out and all in love for God. His unapologetic approach to Truth shines in his storytelling. I have heard these stories before and lived several with him, but his ability to thread them together to ignite action through his testimony is what keeps me smiling to read on. His insights, honesty, and humor are a great recipe for self-reflection. While I have never been much of social media guy, I can say that I have been deep in the pool of social positioning—big house, expensive cars, outspoken comments of 'Where' and 'What' I have been doing and with 'Whom.' I was amazed and drawn in by the facts of it all, or should I say, 'What is real?' or better yet, not real. Thank you, Pastor Rob. Your commitment to help others is your testimony, brother. Keep Going!"

—John Vasquez, CEO, Zivaro Holdings, Inc.

Overliked

Finding Direction, Courage, and
Meaningful Relationships in a Society
Crippled by Social Media

Rob Singleton

GREENLEAF
BOOK GROUP PRESS

Published by Greenleaf Book Group Press
Austin, Texas
www.gbgpress.com

Distributed by Greenleaf Book Group

For ordering information or special discounts for bulk purchases, please contact Greenleaf Book Group at PO Box 91869, Austin, TX 78709, 512.891.6100.

Design and composition by Greenleaf Book Group
Cover design by Greenleaf Book Group
All photos should include a credit line adjacent to the photo:
Image: Thumbs down reluctance, used under license from
Shutterstock.com/©Martial Red

Publisher's Cataloging-in-Publication data is available.

Print ISBN: 978-1-62634-759-5

eBook ISBN: 978-1-62634-760-1

Part of the Tree Neutral® program, which offsets the number of trees consumed in the production and printing of this book by taking proactive steps, such as planting trees in direct proportion to the number of trees used: www.treeneutral.com

TreeNeutral

Printed in the United States of America on acid-free paper

20 21 22 23 24 25   10 9 8 7 6 5 4 3 2 1

First Edition

This book is dedicated to my best friend and partner in crime of over 25 years, my wife, Michelle. Thank you for helping me work through these thoughts and convictions for the last five years and for pressing hard to get this message out!

I also want to dedicate it to my son, Nate, and daughter, Juliana. You both grew up in the middle of the social media tsunami and have learned the good, bad, and ugly from a Gen Z perspective that was much needed. Thank you for your patience with dear old dad!

Contents

Foreword

We are more connected than ever with "what" others are doing. But we are more disconnected than ever with "how" others are doing. We see people, but we don't know people. We observe how they fill their lives, but we are oblivious how empty they might really be. We assume their bright, beautiful pictures mean they have a bright, beautiful life.

And yet, we've all been shocked when a very dark post leaks a very different story into someone's feed. A sudden divorce. A suicide we can't believe. An addiction we can't wrap our minds around. A sharp turn away from their long-held beliefs. A resignation announcing they will be stepping down and stepping away from showing up in your life as they have for years.

The shock of one of those posts gives all who follow them a whiplash emotional experience where we shake our heads and wonder what the real story is and talk about it for a couple of days until a new news story gives us something else to think and talk about. Then we keep scrolling. We just move on. And never quite realize that post should have been a wake-up call to stop simply clicking "like" and instead love people better. To stop just seeing people, observing their lives, and making assumptions. To stop the insanity of following them when they give us what we want but then unfollowing them when they reveal a need or flaw, or how very human their hurting heart really is.

I guess I'm extra sensitive to this because when my marriage blew apart, I watched people shake their heads, wonder what the real story was, and talk about my family as if we were plastic people void of the ability to feel the weight of crushing judgments and stabbing assumptions. I also watched many people quietly disengage from our lives, our problems, because it was easier to walk away than risk some of the mud of our mess getting on them.

I don't fault any of them.

It's hard to deal with our own messes, much less dare to try to help others in theirs. Plus, I'm sure most people assumed we had plenty of help and weren't sure what they could do anyhow.

But the people who did dare to get involved in a loving, kind, understanding way? They saved my life. They helped save my family. And I will never ever be able to thank them enough for daring to go where so few others did.

Rob Singleton is one of those people.

I can't explain to you why Rob did what he did or got involved on the level that he did except to say that he loves Jesus with his whole being and made the choice to heed the call to help us. He didn't keep scrolling past our announcement. He found our phone numbers. He took the risk to call. He dared to listen without making assumptions or judgments or picking sides. He never once uttered, "Well, you know there's always two sides to stories like these"—as if a family falling apart is some sort of spectator sport where you choose a side and cheer for the opposing side to lose.

And he didn't just call once. He kept calling. He kept praying. He kept asking God how he could help. He kept saying yes in whatever way God told him to show up for us. He kept investing time and money—neither of which he had in abundance. And he never stopped during the entire two and a half years my family and I crawled through a tunnel of chaos so dark and so long I wasn't sure I was going to live to see if there really could be light at the end of this tunnel.

As I've looked back on what Rob did, I've often wished he could write a book about what made him stop scrolling and start deeply investing the way he did. How did he change the optics on our situation and start seeing a hope we couldn't even see for ourselves? How did he find the motivation to keep believing, keep reaching out, and keep pressing in to help a family with whom he had no blood relationship at all? How did he escape the "like" mentality of social media to truly love people as God wants us all to do?

And I guess the biggest question of all, how can I be more of a Rob in other people's stories? Granted, we can't be deeply invested in every person's life we follow on social media. But what if we dared to ask God to show us some people who need us to go beyond just liking a post and scrolling on? And what if we stopped believing the lie that there are plenty of others helping them and just found the courage to start somewhere with helping them? And what if God uses us as he used Rob in our lives?

I can't speak for others, but I can tell you what Rob's investment meant to us. Though we had every strike against us and very few people thought we'd make it, we did. Today, I looked across our front yard and watched my husband playing with my three grandkids. He was laughing. He was healthy. He was engaged and truly happy to be with these little people climbing all over him and begging him to throw them in the air one more time.

Then Art smiled over at me.

That smile was worth more to me than all the money in the world. It said, "You are safe, Lysa. We are safe." So, I snapped a picture. It's not one I'll ever post on Instagram. After all, it's far too priceless to let the world decide whether or not to like it. It's just for me and Art. And I'll probably also frame it and send it to Rob with a note of thanks to the man who decided truly loving people is so much more of a worthy pursuit then simply clicking "like."

Thank you for being so brave, Rob. May we all seek to be a little more like the Jesus in you.

—Lysa TerKeurst

Read First

I don't make friends that easily. I want to. I actually love making friends. Relationships are at the heart of everything that I do. But I'm no Dale Carnegie, so this book isn't subtitled "How to Win Friends and Influence People." Nevertheless, I am passionate about people. So when social media came along, I was an early adopter. I saw it as a possible shortcut to connect with people without having to worry about whether I had a subconscious smirk on my face, lettuce in my teeth, or one of those resting _itch faces alluded to so often in social media. *More conversations? Sign me up!* The minute a shiny new social media innovation flew by, I grabbed it. And I confess: it was fun to watch my lists of "friends" grow exponentially. "Take THAT, mocking trolls!" So I wholeheartedly embraced the new, expanded world of "friends" and "followers." It's amazing, right?

Let's face it—technology is *enjoyable.* I'd never want to go back to Downton Abbey days, nor do I believe our tech advances are ushering in a dystopian Mad Max future. We're somewhere between those two. It's a great time to be alive. At what other time in world history could you become proficient at something *without getting out of your pajamas?*

We can connect with people all over the planet. We can share our thoughts, goals, ideas, and feelings on every subject with everyone, anytime we want. And we can get feedback in real time, all the time . . . *whether we want it or not.*

I love what we can do with technology. But . . .

Some of us are starting to sense that something is wrong, even if we can't pinpoint what it is.

Yes, it's *great* to be alive today. Yet, it can feel *fake* to be alive today. Sometimes that virtual connectedness can leave us feeling completely disconnected and alone.

I found out the hard way how relationships with "friends and followers" can get very sideways, very fast.

My "friends and followers" story started with eight people in my living room. We were a group of people who cared deeply for each other and shared a dream of bringing love to our city.

Over the next few years, my family and our closest friends built a large church. At the core of that church was Jesus Christ and a web of closely connected relationships and friendships. Our love for each other spilled over into our city. I'd had a chaotic childhood littered with broken friendships and instability, so this experience was completely new for me. It felt like what connection was meant to be.

I officiated at weddings, blessed babies, buried parents. I talked with folks for thousands of hours, listening to their deepest concerns and hurts. I loved helping them. My family shoveled dirt, dug ditches, painted walls, and served all sorts of people. As a group, we worked in relief efforts after catastrophes like Hurricane Katrina in New Orleans and the earthquake in Haiti. It was the most satisfying thing my wife and I had ever done. We loved the people we worked with—the people we served—and they loved us back.

For 17 years, these folks encouraged me, letting me know that I gave them insight and perspective on a weekly basis. They said we helped them live better and more spiritual lives. Those words always astonished and humbled me. Their friendship enriched my life. And isn't that what we all want? To be needed, appreciated, and loved? To be a part of something bigger and more beautiful than ourselves? I felt like the unlikely hero in my own story. It was an incredibly fulfilling season in our lives.

But I also had a feeling that my time at the church was wrapping up. I wanted them to be prepared, to be able to stand on their own feet if I was not there, so I shared this with my leadership team (in retrospect, maybe not my smartest move). Then I left for a month to seek the Lord and to get clarity. But before I did, I confronted a member of the church leadership team who had been caught time and time again acting unethically and hurtfully toward others. I told him that he needed to clean it up before I got back (in retrospect, *definitely* not my smartest move).

While I was away, instead of cleaning up, he covered up and enlisted others to help him. They met regularly, like some sort of shadow government—only this wasn't a conspiracy theory; it was all too real. In those meetings they were crafting a script to alienate me from my team using hints of chaos, half-truths, and fake news. I was clueless about this while I was away. In the meantime, gossip spread. It was crazy talk, like I had murdered someone's pet unicorn or faked a moon landing. But gossiping can feel good. I get that. People become addicted, and the lies grow and spread. Pretty soon even close friends seemed more willing to believe I was a drug lord overseeing a cartel rather than the same God-fearing, Christ-centered pastor they'd known for years. Not a shred of evidence then or now, but the trust people had in me seemed deeply damaged.

When I got back, I found I'd been unfriended, unliked, and even blocked by people—including dear friends—I'd known for years. Before this, I might have moaned about a bad haircut, but the difference between a bad haircut and a good haircut is only about two weeks. By contrast, this was excruciating. It went on and on. It felt like a bad breakup . . . a divorce with thousands of people. These people were my family. I can hardly think about it now without tearing up.

Have you ever had a relationship implode like that? I'd been blindsided. It was like a nightmare . . . except that I was awake. I didn't recognize my own life. Where had the years of love and connection gone? There was nothing I could say or do without making myself look guilty. I sat in my house, surrounded by a city of people I'd considered friends, feeling completely alone. There were very few people I could trust or even dare talk to. All that we had worked to accomplish together, all the goodness, the love, the hope . . . was gone. *After all this time together, didn't they know the real me?*

Apparently not.

And that may have been difficult for me to accept at the time, but facts are pesky and persistent things—and, as I've heard it said, "Facts don't care about your feelings." Offered an alternative narrative, those who did not really know me past the Sunday sermon reacted like good boys and girls at suppertime who always eat whatever is set before them, no questions asked. However, what was being served wasn't a healthy serving of vegetables but more like twinkies and diet soda—fun to eat but damaging in the long run. Looked good. Tasted good. Wasn't good.

Solomon warned us about this stuff in Proverbs 18:7–8: *"The mouths of fools are their undoing, and their lips are a snare to their very lives. The words of a gossip are like choice morsels; they go down to the inmost parts"* (emphasis added).

While I was away, wolves had crept in unnoticed. Actually, they *were* noticed—it's just that they presented "sheep optics" rather than "wolf optics." And all the while, they flashed their reassuring smiles; few seemed to take note of the fact that sheep don't have fangs.

As we read in Romans 12:19, Amplified Bible (AMP), "Beloved, never avenge yourselves, but leave the way open for God's wrath [and his judicial righteousness]; for it is written [in scripture], 'Vengeance is Mine, I will repay,' says the Lord."

All this being said, brace yourself for the blunt truth in three . . . two . . . one . . .

Life's not fair!

Don't just blow by that statement. The failure to come to terms with it has ruined countless lives. And even though we all probably realize this deep down inside, it doesn't hurt to keep reminding ourselves—so I'll say it again.

Life's not fair.

And this truth's second cousin also bears reminding, "The concept of 'fair' isn't even all that useful."

For instance, the most powerful person for the last 100 years or so is usually considered to be the president of the United States. Yet, even the president can be treated unfairly—and often is. So let me ask you something: Does crying "Unfair! Unfair!" ever really change things? The word *unfair* may have been among the most tweeted words during one former president's administration, but it may also have been the least effective. And that's because, as I said earlier, the concept of fair isn't even really useful in our current cultural climate.

Why?

Because much of the "unfairness" that happens in the world is not within our control. And if that's the case, how productive is it to fume about what's fair and unfair? Quoting author Jonathan Lockwood Huie, "'Fair' is not a useful concept. Life is not 'fair.' You can't make life 'fair.' You can get angry. You can complain about life not being 'fair.' You can attempt revenge—perhaps violently. You can inflict great suffering upon yourself in the name of life being 'unfair.' And life is still not 'fair.'"[1]

Add to this the fact that negativity tends to boomerang. This is because of what psychologists call "trait transference," whereby the qualities you use to describe other people become associated with *you*. So if you're always criticizing and casting shade on other people, folks come to see you under the very same shadow.

In other words, it turns out there's really something to that old childhood chant: "I'm rubber, and you're glue. Whatever you say bounces off me and sticks to you!"

Outside, I kept smiling, trying to make the best of it, encouraging people that everything was going to be great. But inside, my heart had been ripped out. I could not believe it. They all . . . *hated* me? Really?

That eight-person dream that started in my living room and blossomed into an amazing community came to a heart-rending end. Forget defending myself—I became too discouraged for that, or to confront the lies. Besides, it was like playing a social game of Whac-a-Mole—no sooner would I knock one down than three more would pop up. It didn't take long for me to feel the truth of the old saying, "A lie travels halfway around the world before the truth even puts its boots on."

Most of us have experienced this when we find ourselves defending misinformation or slander that seems to have rocket boosters while the truth is like a 100-year-old lady crossing the street with her walker—it takes f-o-r-e-v-e-r! But while most have come to accept this, few ever consider why. I discuss this in a later section about truth.

But back then, fear, insecurity, and anxiety gripped me. And these things were to be my constant companions over the next several months.

My family and I eventually moved on and moved away. Getting away from those former friends gave me a new perspective. Slowly but surely, I felt myself climbing out of an emotional darkness.

My gift had always been the ability to share insights and perspectives to help others navigate their lives. It is the thing I love doing. Helping people feeds my soul. I started with that. Wherever people would listen to me, I tried to help. I met with people who were struggling. 1 built an online group of followers, sharing encouragement. Lots of likes. Lots of great feedback. Lots of thumbs-ups. This was good, right? I was moving on. I was getting past the shattering pain and betrayal and finally healing. I thought it was working.

All through the ordeal, my family stood by me. Now, as I grasped at what might be a new life, they reached with me. But they weren't buying into my forced happy posts and polished one-liners. They saw through my upbeat online personas. All the filtered photos in the world couldn't fool them into thinking I was actually completely healed.

One day, my children came to me, together with my wife, and challenged me. They said, "You hardly laugh anymore. You're irritated with us all the time. You get mad easily. You used to be fun.

Now you're a drag. We don't think you've healed. We want our old dad back."

Ouch.

My first thought was *Wha—???* My optics were great! I had a good group of followers again. I felt as though I was once more doing what I was good at—helping people. My life had restarted. People liked me! I was accepted! I was a hero again! But now, I was devastated (. . . again). *Not even my own family likes me?*

That was the final kick in the gut that started me down a decade-long path that has brought me to this book. After the lies and mistrust tore down what I had worked hard to build up, I was desperate to be accepted again. I was eager to rebuild a faith community. But rather than doing the hard work of rebuilding within myself, where I was hurting, I simply put up a happy facade. It was like building a foundation on sand instead of bedrock. I had been caught playing a game and acting as if it were real life.

My kids were right in far too many ways. I had become a pretender, a phony, a hypocrite. I wanted to help others, but I couldn't even help myself. My family loved me enough to tell me the truth. And believe me, I know all about faking it.

When I was a child, my family moved 22 times before I was 19 years old. Twenty-two times I had to smile and say, "Hi, my name is Rob. I have two parents and an older brother and sister." In fifth grade alone, I repeated that line three times in three different schools. I reinvented myself on a regular basis. I grew up knowing the difference between real and pretend. But the trap was still so easy to fall into.

The truth was, if I wanted my heart to mend, I was going to have to be real. I had to embrace authenticity with all its messiness. Fake likes and thumbs-ups weren't going to mend the hurt in my heart. Pseudo-relationships and virtual pats on the back weren't going to satiate my deep hunger for connection and relationship. "Friends and followers" weren't enough.

They weren't enough for me. And they're not enough for you.

This book isn't pointing a finger at anyone whose life has become less than authentic. It's pointing a finger at *how easily* I slipped from authentic, loving relationships into an artificial life. It's pointing a finger so we can look in that direction and see what we need to avoid.

This book isn't anti-technology; it's pro-authenticity. Think of it as being pro-*you*—*the real you*.

This book isn't saying social media is bad. It's saying *the real you is better.* You matter more than any image. You're more worthy of love than any avatar you could ever create.

This book is also not saying *you* have a problem. I'm saying *I had a problem.*

And I'm saying that being a performance-driven, optics-oriented fraud is a very easy trap to fall into. *I'm convinced it can happen to anyone.*

When we fall into the trap, we lose our ability to have normal emotions of joy, pain, gratitude, even love. We quit being fun. We don't laugh easily, we're preoccupied, and any enjoyment becomes forced and fake.

We also tend to go into what I call *safety mode* in order to protect our social image. In this posture we shy away from writing or saying *anything* that might reduce the value of our avatar—anything that might blur the optics of our otherwise clearly compliant, unobjectionable (in any way) image we've so carefully crafted. And we choose instead to tweet the right narrative, type the right hashtags, or post the correct daily virtue signal—such as some did when they made sure their Instagram or TikTok went dark for blackout Tuesday. It's estimated that over 20 million posted the now famous black square, but what few realize is that for most of them, that's the most they'll ever do for the cause. Listen, I get it; action is needed. But it can't be executed for its own sake effectively.

But reconnecting with authentic relationships—starting with our relationship with ourselves—renews us. It rekindles the fire inside, rebuilds our confidence, and releases the toxins that may have come from people who didn't "like" us or who "unliked" us.

Finding the way to close relationships, to connections that work, to fulfillment and joy and a great life is possible for *everyone*. This book is a pathway to being, and continuing to be, the real, true, authentic *you*.

Read This Too

A t the end of each chapter, you'll have an opportunity to contemplate everything that has been discussed in a special (optional) section called *A Change of Heart*.

A Change of Heart will help cement the discoveries you have made in each chapter, so you can apply them in real life.

If we are looking for authenticity, love, and real relationships, we are going to need to change our perspective and anchor ourselves in life-changing truth. We can carve time out of our busy lives to reflect on and respond to that truth in our own hearts.

Each *Change of Heart* section includes an invitation to *think, pause, connect,* and *respond.*

Think: Remember discoveries in that chapter; anchor yourself in truth and authenticity.

Pause: Take time to ask important questions; reflect on the state of your own heart in light of the truth.

Connect: Connect to an ancient truth that will encourage your heart and build out a new way of thinking and living.

Respond: Start a conversation with God—the one who created true authentic love and relationship.

Chapter 1

What Is Real?

'm racing full speed, trees blurring past on both sides, wind cutting across my face. I'm sure it's the fastest I've ever skied. I schuss down the hill to the bottom, where I set an edge and swerve to a stop in a spray of snow. I grew up downhill racing from age 16 to 18, and I know from the feel how fast I was going. I am pretty sure this was my most epic run. Okay, at least in the last 10 years. The stop wasn't all bad either. I pull off my goggles and catch my breath, furtively glancing to see if anyone saw what I just did, instinctively looking for phones in people's hands. I also throw together a few quick thoughts in my head for the obligatory and ever so humble "Who me?" speech sure to be requested.

Standing there, catching my breath, I'm thinking, *Man! Did I just do that? This had to be my best run in years.* Then, after I look around, I'm thinking, *Are you kidding me? No cameras?* Then I spot him, one teenager clapping his hands, stopping to motion to me, then clapping his hands again. I pull off my earbuds to hear what he wants. He says, "Dude, you were shredding!" And I say what we would *all* say in that situation, *"Did you video it?"* Nope.

Elation turns to disappointment, and I head over to the lodge. Inwardly, I'm trusting that one of my friends or family saw me on the run. But no one did. Not even a shaky GoPro validating my awesomeness. I'm alone in my awesomeness. *Why didn't I get that kid's name and number?* I would have paid him to come by my table that night at dinner and say, *"Wait! Aren't you that beast that destroyed Breckenridge today?!"* Instead, that night at dinner, I had to say it myself, and it lost all effect. My family had to take my word for it, and now you do too. Please believe me. I went fast.

Two days later, I'm on a much smaller run with slushy snow. I turn to look at my son and . . . My. Ski. Stops. One minute I am upwardly mobile, the next I am upwardly gazing. Freak dumb rookie accident. I'm moaning in pain as I grab my leg. *What just happened?* I look around for help and also . . . to see if anyone saw me. *Did anybody video that?* The thought is a little ego-shattering. I see someone with a phone in his hand, but I'm not sure if the camera is on. Then I realize he's calling the ski patrol. Ski patrol! In no time flat, I'm being carried down the hill. On a stretcher! You know what I'm thinking: *If anyone catches this, it's never getting posted. I refuse to be reduced to a meme! Or worse, a gif!*

These days, cameras are pointed at all of us, everywhere—from grocery stores to signal lights to strangers in crowds. I'm a professional guy who is secure in my identity, with a family and a big enough circle of friends to feel loved even when I do something dumb. So if being "liked" or "videoed" or "shared" can still inflate or deflate me, what does it do to the people who have all their digital "friends"—and enemies—watching *and commenting* about them on social media *all* the time? Are we really more concerned with how we perform virtually than in real life? For many of us, the unfortunate answer is yes.

Social media blunders can be *devastating.* That ski fall tore my ACL, but at least my image, my identity, and my self-respect stayed intact. What do you do if they don't? What if your mood rises and falls according to those images and interactions that appear after the fact? There should be a vaccine against the deflation of our own attitudes, a cure for negative reactions when online "relationships" turn ugly. *And there is . . .*

Getting Real about Connection

"I enjoy feeling lonely, disconnected, and unloved," said no one ever.

In a world divided by economics, political views, and gender roles, there are a few foundational truths that we can all agree on. *Love is life-giving. And authentic relationships matter greatly.* Almost everyone would agree to that.

The connection with those whom we love shapes everything from our self-confidence to our grade point average. In a survey of over 20,000 adults ages 18–64, rating the most important aspects of life, the top two answers were (1) friends and family and (2) a happy relationship.[1] At the core of our being, we long for solid ties, love-filled relationships, and lifelong friendships. We need each other. Our ability to connect with those around us defines how we see ourselves, how we succeed in our work, and how we feel about life.

The problem is, in this age of instant, global connection, we are somehow becoming more and more disconnected. It is becoming increasingly difficult for people to be themselves and reveal what's really going on in their lives. To a large degree, this is because the lines are being blurred between real and authentic and what's politically correct and preapproved to say out loud or even online. Our ability to engage with those around us seems to be faltering. It is becoming easy to confuse the notion of being "connected" with being in actual relationship.

As a global village, we are certainly more networked. Well over 60 percent of the world's population has cell phones.[2] But we are also more isolated. Oddly, the generation that was all but born with a device in their hand is feeling this isolation more than previous ones. While 90 percent of millennials engage regularly in social media, 22 percent say they have no friends at all.[3] Read that again. Not "few real friends" but "no friends at all." Well, I guess there's a silver lining—at least they can still tell the difference. However, that's hardly comforting in light of the fact that we are creatures of community who lack any kind of real community.

Orthodox Christianity teaches the biblical truth that God is one with three distinct personalities—the Father, Son, and Holy Spirit. It's called the Trinity. In the first book of the Bible, Genesis, we also learn that humankind was God's crowning achievement. He said in Genesis 1:31 that it was "very good." Not just "good" but "very good." Back up a few verses and we see why. In Genesis 1:27 it says, "So God created mankind in his own image. . . . " And what is one of the main things about the image of God? That he is one God in three persons. In other words, *community.*

> **"The generation that was all but born with a device in their hand is feeling this isolation more than previous ones."**

Let me put this another way. We were made for community *by* community. The fall from grace marred that image, and ever since there's been this tension between trying to be our own gods and following the God who made us. And though it would take an entire book just to talk about this one truth (several books, actually), our focus is this one aspect of community. Since we're made for community and are creatures of community (and BTW, even those who don't have a Christian worldview accept this reality, as countless psychological studies attest), then it logically follows that a constant and deliberate effort to isolate ourselves both virtually and physically will ultimately undermine our emotional and spiritual health.

Millennials between ages 18 and 24 are four times more likely to feel lonely "most of the time" compared to people over 70.[4] Overall suicide rates dropped steadily until 2007 but have since climbed.[5] A letter written by Juli Wilson almost broke the internet after her husband, Jarrid, a mental health advocate, committed suicide.[6] Jarrid wrote a tremendous book called *Jesus Swagger* to challenge readers by asking if they were real or just posing, specifically calling out fraudulent Christians. I have the greatest respect for the man, his family, and his book. I bring up his memory to illustrate that the dilemma about authenticity is real, it's deadly, and we have to find a way out of its alluring trap.

The rampant disconnection between people and others, even the disconnection people feel inside themselves, underscores a troubling aspect of technology: it is designed to help you go wide but not deep. We're seeing more and more people who have 500-plus Facebook friends but no one to hang out with on the weekends. We can have 1,000 Instagram followers and yet feel utterly alone.

The Connection Disconnection

At no other time in history have we had such rapid access to each other. With a phone call, a text, or a video chat, the people we love and care about are virtually at our fingertips. In the coronavirus crisis that stopped the world, people were able to stay in regular communication with each other. A recent international study shows that most people spend 41 percent of each day in front of a screen, whether it's a phone, tablet, TV, or computer.[7] We turn to our ever-present handheld devices to connect with those around us. The technology that links us together is amazing.

However, the issue of disconnection isn't the technology, but our use of it and how our brains filter what's being taken in. Our perception of reality becomes skewed as we scroll through our Instagram feed or view the latest posts on Facebook.

Our online connectivity has changed our relational behaviors. We "friend" and "unfriend" with the tap of a screen. We decide if life is good based on if we are *liked* on Facebook (and by *liked*, I am referring to the virtual thumbs-up) or "followed" on Instagram.

Unfortunately, the importance of whether our latest post is "liked" can outweigh the importance of us being *liked* ourselves.

That vital connection we long for is too often displaced by the need for validation, a thumbs-up, smiley face, wink face, thank-you hands, heart emoji, fire emoji . . . take your pick—I got more! That real life-giving love we are actually longing for is constantly being replaced in favor of accumulating likes. Our desire to be liked is so oversaturated we've reached a point of being "overliked."

Researchers at aerospace and defense manufacturer Northrop Grumman state that the lure of *likes* on social media literally rewires our brains.[8] Each time one of our posts receives a *like*, it fires off a hit of dopamine. Dopamine is a neurotransmitter in the brain, a chemical messenger, that helps us feel pleasure. According to Northrop Grumman, getting a *like* online "triggers the same kind of chemical reaction that is caused by gambling and recreational drugs." The evidence seems irrefutable. But maybe you need more proof. I warn you, this next tidbit is pretty humbling.

Harvard University researchers learned that self-disclosure on social media lights up the brain just the same as addictive chemicals.[9] The Addiction Center reported that the brain's reward centers "are most active when people are talking about themselves."[10] On social media, people talk about themselves 80 percent of the time, but if you were talking in real life, it would be only 30 to 40 percent. When people reveal themselves and get a "like," it perpetuates the social media habit. Duck lips anyone? Selfish much? 'Nough said— we're addicted to *likes*.

> "Unfortunately, the importance of whether our latest post is 'liked' can outweigh the importance of us being *liked* ourselves."

Overlooked or Overliked?

If it seems like the case I'm attempting to lay out is heavily weighted toward our selfish tendencies to want everything, all the time, to be about us, I've got good news. That's only half of it. The other half is our fear of being overlooked. And the two of these dysfunctions together are worse than the one-two combination of Mike Tyson in his prime. It bears a little closer look.

So stay with me on this as we go just a little further down the rabbit hole. My intention is not to depress you or instill a sense of hopelessness about living in a social media–saturated society. As I said earlier, that ship has sailed. However, the diagnosis varies dramatically between those with an "if you can't beat 'em, join 'em" mentality and those who have found freedom and broken the S&M chains (social and media—what were you thinking?).

The majority of this book is about that communal promised land of real fellowship and authentic relationships, but unlike the Israelites, who failed to cross the Jordan River and enter the promised land the first go-around, we are going to have to cross over God's way. Period. So let's see if we can bring this home.

Let's start with the word *like*.

Like is a versatile word. It's a verb. *I like you.* A preposition. *The road was slick like butter.* A conjunction. *My toe hurts like crazy.* A slang adverb. *That was, like, crazy.* And now, most importantly, a noun. As in, *how many likes did you get on that post?* (Yes, you guessed it. I found an English teacher to write this paragraph for me.)[11]

Like it or not, social media is shaping our culture and our conversations. For many people and companies, it is shaping our careers. After Kylie Jenner tweeted that she didn't use Snapchat anymore, the value plummeted, costing the company $1.3 billion (with a *b*).[12] Taylor Swift (and probably every celebrity alive) gauges what she'll post or not post based on likes.[13]

Celebrity influencers can pull up to $1 million for ad space on their feeds.[14] Nonprofit companies are launched by crowd-sourcing apps. Careers are destroyed by poorly crafted posts. Even the "serious" news is affected. Today, social media outstrips traditional newsprint as a source of world events. And . . . Baby Yoda has gone viral.[15] (Who *doesn't* love a space baby with supernatural powers?)

Likes are powerful. Superpowerful.

And as for the social media industry? *Likes* mean money.

Tech companies are concerned with *networking* more than *relationship*. At the end of the day, these tech companies are for-profit corporations. They have demands from their stakeholders to have rapid growth predominantly by means of advertising dollars. Advertisers spend money when eyes view their content or click on their product links. *The more eyes, the more money. You may not be concerned about the money linked to your viewing habits . . . but that is what most concerns social media companies. The status of your relationships and personal connectivity doesn't even cross their corporate radar.*

Social media is influencing our offline relationships, too. In the past three years, I have been increasingly involved in conversations where the other party is referencing something they saw on social media. Remember? Our online activities influence our brains, our concept of who we are, and our behavior, but that's far from where it ends. Eventually, it spills over into our homes and hearts. We need to think critically about how we are using this technology.

While the original concept of social media was to provide a way for people to stay connected to each other, we're seeing more and more developments that make social media more and more impersonal. *Likes* have even made their way into our private chats, texts, and emails. Now, instead of responding with words, you can simply click the thumb to *like* a message. This impersonal feature can amplify the anxiety users are already facing regarding being ignored or disregarded.

Relationships are defined with the click of a button. Just don't be the guy who clicks the wrong button. Former US Representative Anthony Weiner famously revealed his "sexting" habit when he accidentally used his public Twitter account to send a picture of his privates to a college student.[16] He was forced to resign. Perhaps coincidentally, the next year Merriam-Webster added the word *sexting* to the official dictionary.[17]

Admission

Everything shows up online now. News of baby births and deaths of loved ones are shared via post. Critical conversations become sound bites. Our "emotional invisibility" enables us to say and do things we would never say or do in a face-to-face exchange. We've all seen the online disagreements and outright fights between strangers who have never even met.

On a national level, a former president of the United States tweeted on-demand thoughts at any time. Half-formed thoughts got the presidential seal of approval, and millions of people consumed them. (That kind of reach is both cool . . . and scary at the same time.)

The world is literally at our fingertips . . . and we are voting with our likes. In this age of information and optics, a *like* is a public stamp of approval. A virtual representation of your worth. When I *like* your post or your feed, I validate who you are. *I see you.* And subsequently, my lack of likes can leave you feeling unseen and dismissed. *You don't think so?* Just recall the last time a post or picture went unnoticed on your feed.

> **"In this age of information and optics, a *like* is a public stamp of approval. A virtual representation of your worth."**

My skiing buddy Brandon called me recently for advice. He and his wife, Melissa, were concerned about their best friends. The couples vacationed together, raised kids together. It was that kind of friendship. But the wife of the couple had become an "influencer" and was now so involved in herself that she'd distanced herself, and her husband, from everyone. Brandon asked me how to approach his friend about his wife's problem. He said, "She's so caught up in getting 'likes' from strangers that she doesn't seem to care about the real people right in front of her. She's just a 'persona,' and her husband's a sidekick. Sure, she's buying the groceries, but it's killing us." Brandon and Melissa were heartbroken to lose their best friends because of "likes."

Those little pixelated thumbs-ups and heart emojis help shape not only people's self-esteem but also their connections to the outside world. By the outside world, I mean the 3.45 billion people who engage in social media each day.

The real question is . . . do people *like* you or not?

Social Goggles

Instead of rose-colored glasses, we now view the world through social goggles. Instead of defining our worth by who we are, we have learned to define our worth by how we're seen by others, by who likes us . . . or not. That is a whole lot of power to give to a bunch of avatars. Yep. The people you are hoping will validate your existence . . . aren't real. The influencers, the game changers, even your coworker who recently friended you on LinkedIn, whoever they are online . . . is not who they are in real life.

Admit it . . . neither are you. The *you* that you reveal to the world via Instagram or on Facebook is rarely the real you. It is a carefully crafted avatar, with curated content, filtered photos, and edited dialogue. A patchwork of your best moments, your coolest vacations, your highlight reels, and your snappiest social commentary. With the power of technology, you are crafting the person that you long to be. The person who has it all together. Or should I say, the *persona* that has it all together.

People from my parents' generation recall being afraid that someone might watch them, or that they'd be caught by surprise on camera. Today, young people *expect* it. In fact, the disorder called *scopophobia* is the fear of being seen.[18] Today, it's listed by one writer as one of the 10 weirdest phobias that exists, right up there with the fear of the pope (papaphobia), the fear of peanut butter (arachibutyrophobia), and the fear of teenagers (ephebiphobia). Who could imagine being afraid of any of that? Well, I suppose sometimes that teenager one . . .

However, one weird phobia is on the rise. It's called *nomophobia*, the fear of being without a mobile device or without cell phone coverage.[19] It's as frightening as a trip to the dentist or "wedding day jitters." *Psychology Today* reports that 65 percent of Americans sleep with their phones beside them, and more than half never switch them off. And all jokes aside, 34 percent of Americans answer their cell phones even during times of intimacy with their partner (thus revealing which "like" they value more), and a growing number of college students even shower with their cell phones.

Even though a growing body of research indicates that people who spend more time on their screens are unhappier than those who are not tethered to their phones, we all tend to *live* ready. Our phones at our sides, our finger on our camera button, our face ready to . . . thrust neck out, put tongue on roof of mouth, and *smize*, like Tyra taught us. We know what is likeable, and we do all we can to achieve that standard with each communication. Our brains are looking for that next dopamine hit. Our hearts are consumed with how we look—almost as though "how we look" will transform our heart. But God's word makes it clear that this transformation works not from the outside in, but rather the inside out. Proverbs 15:13 says, "A joyful heart makes a cheerful face. But when the heart is sad, the spirit is broken." So it would seem that rather than continuing with hearts consumed with how we look, we should be consumed with developing our hearts because a joyful heart has a more transforming effect on how we look than any filter or photoshopping ever could.

What we believe, value, and long for all seep out in our methodical, carefully timed online revelations. Whether you realize it or not, you have a different identity online. It is the "super" you.

Superhero Cape . . . or Invisibility Cloak?

The movie *Avengers: Endgame* brought in over $1 billion in its first five days in theaters.[20] Unbelievable. While I love the Marvel Cinematic Universe as much as the next guy, it is literally *unbelievable*. I mean, when you think about a Norse god with golden locks who can call down lightning and save the world with a special hammer . . . well, it's not very realistic.

Yet, we love the idea of butt-kicking superheroes. There is no reality behind the myth. No one came out of that movie thinking they were going to run into Captain America grabbing coffee or fly off to Wakanda for the weekend. Superheroes don't exist. Superpowers are not a thing. No matter how fun they are in the stories we love, they don't exist in real life.

Whether we realize it or not, our social media avatars are as fake as those superheroes on the screen. Our photos are scrubbed, cropped, and photoshopped. Our style is cool and eclectic. We don't take a selfie in the mirror to show how bad we look when we roll out of bed on Saturday morning . . . or afternoon. Our family pics don't show conflict or stress. Except when they do. Then we end up on AwkwardFamilyPhotos.com.

When we do decide to share something "authentic" or "real"

online, it almost never is. Our emotions, happy or sad, are portrayed in a way to invite feedback. There is just one problem. None of it is real. And in our quest for relationship and love? It is difficult to find real connection when everything about us . . . is fake.

We lose the real story of who we are when we curate ourselves for the benefit of others. And we get so busy watching the special effects in other people's lives that we forget to look for the reality behind them. While we are desperately hoping that the "superhero" we are portraying is making us more likeable, the opposite effect is happening. In real life, social media can make us invisible. This is a strange statement, since the potential audience for our online interactions is *huge*. Allow me to explain.

> "We lose the real story of who we are when we curate ourselves for the benefit of others."

When we post, we are essentially putting our online "friends" in charge of making our voices heard. Rather than talking directly to those close to us about the ins and outs of our days, we essentially shout into the void with a Facebook status or a tweet.

The challenge is that hundreds of thousands of "voices" are shouting at the same time we are. InternetLiveStats.com shows how many posts are created on social media platforms in real time. This ranges from several thousand to hundreds of thousands every second. The void gets exponentially larger by the minute. The chances of our voices being heard among the crowd grows infinitely smaller moment by moment. All the social chatter can leave us feeling unseen and unheard.

Exchanging personal interactions with impersonal posts on social media has a cost. Giving the power to validate or invalidate our thoughts to the online community can take a huge toll on our self-esteem. That's why cyberbullying is so damnable. Cyberbullying has been directly linked to teen suicides doubling between 2008 and 2015.[21]

Confusion, Fear, and Disconnection

Instead of finding a vibrant community online, we find ourselves awash in a sea of negative emotions. Instead of fostering connection, social media tends to foster competition . . . comparison . . . jealousy . . . anxiety . . . with a side of FOMO (fear of missing out). These emotions lead people to do crazy things. One woman has created 150 of the same outfits worn by Princess Kate (but looks nothing like the princess in them).[22] Many women make themselves look like Barbie dolls. One has racked up 1.2 million followers; another racked up 36 plastic surgeries.[23] And FOMO is real, creating lower levels of life satisfaction.[24] People with FOMO live in a vicious cycle of being driven to check social media more often, and then "up the ante" on whatever or whoever they perceive as being ahead of them in the make-believe race they've entered, all of which only increases their FOMO. Which, BTW, is nothing new. FOMO is what the tempter used in the early chapters of Genesis in order to get the first man and woman to doubt God—or to suspect that they were missing out on something God wanted to keep for himself. Pretty incredible when you consider that it doesn't get any better than paradise! Yet that's how powerful FOMO can be.

It is obvious that the onslaught of online content can leave us confused and completely disconnected from the reality of the world around us. *Psychology Today* says that we often subtly substitute virtual relationships for the real flesh-and-blood connections that we so desperately need.[25] Why is our mental and emotional state so closely linked to our social media use?

Many studies have been conducted regarding the effects of social media on self-esteem, but they all seem to point to the same thing: *the more time a person spends on social media, the lower their self-esteem.* [26]

Lower self-esteem is commonly attributed to the fact that social media users feel as if they're (1) being overlooked and (2) developing an intense tendency to compare themselves to others.[27] This mental anguish seems a little contradictory compared to the promised joy of all those "friends" and followers, right? Shallow relationships, negative emotions, and the insatiable need for validation are a toxic cocktail.

Even those influencers who have gathered millions of followers struggle with feelings of depression and anxiety. If you achieve your goal of global success online, the constant pressure to maintain metrics and numbers can be crippling. A perfectly curated feed often hides feelings of inadequacy and inner struggles. Summer, a 20-year-old lifestyle vlogger with a million followers, says that viewers often see YouTubers as characters in a show instead of real people.[28] The kind of constant scrutiny they endure doesn't bring fulfillment; it makes them feel fake. In a hilarious illustration of this, *Aquaman* star Jason Momoa did a Super Bowl ad where he unwinds at home by taking off foot-tall shoes, all his muscles, and his hair. The commercial screamed, *Fake fake fake!* And no one was shocked—after all, it was supposed to be shocking. But far from being funny because it was so far-fetched, it was only mildly amusing because it's been done a million times. And yet, we go on trying to curate perfect content, all the while knowing it won't curate a perfect life. Isn't that the street definition of insanity? Doing the same thing over and over again and expecting different results?

Speaking of insanity, social media companies are taking notice of the mental health issues caused by online use. Some are testing ways to hide these negative emotion triggers and improve customer experience by removing the opportunity to compare (i.e., eliminating likes).[29] If the big guns are seeing the negative trends of comparison and anxiety, shouldn't we?

Social media may be making us another face in the online crowd, but we still have the power to make our voices heard. We don't have to buy into the belief that our self-worth is linked to our viewership. We can make a shift from virtual connection to real relationships. We can take the leap from fake *likes* to real love.

> "We don't have to buy into the belief that our self-worth is linked to our viewership. We can make a shift from virtual connection to real relationships. We can take the leap from fake *likes* to real love."

Clarity, Courage, and Connection

In a world of incessant online chatter and social invisibility, you need to know that you are not alone. You can have real connection and vital friendships. You can break free from your social media dopamine hits and your "superhero" avatar. You don't have to present yourself in a certain way to be who you truly are. Your highlight reel isn't the real you. You don't have to get every detail right to have value. Your worth is not intrinsically linked to your view count.

The good news is, the real, authentic you can find purpose, relationship, and wholeness.

A vibrant, healthy, fulfilling life is what we get when we embrace the real person we were created to be. So let's get going. Let me help you change the optics.

A CHANGE OF HEART

At the core of our being, we long for solid ties, love-filled relationships, and lifelong friendships. We need each other.

THINK

- At its best, social media engagement can connect us in amazing ways with those we love and care for. At its worst, it leaves us feeling invisible and alone as we shout into the void.

- Superhero avatars cannot validate our self-worth and emotions. We can lose the real story of who we are when we curate ourselves for the benefit of others.

- The real, authentic you can find purpose, relationship, and wholeness.

- We can make a shift from virtual connection to real relationships. We can take the leap from fake *likes* to real love.

PAUSE

- How do your interactions on social media influence how you see yourself? Are you addicted to *likes*?

- Are you jealous of your friends due to the pressure of FOMO as you scroll through your feed? How does it impact your friendships with those people?

- How does your curated feed hide your inner struggles and hurts?

- What would your daily life look like if you invested more time in face-to-face relationships instead of interacting online?

CONNECT

Teach me your ways, O Lord, that I may live according to your truth! Grant me purity of heart, so that I may honor you. (Psalm 86:11, NLT)

RESPOND

God, I want real, authentic relationships in my life. I am tired of trying to be someone I can't be. I want my heart grounded in real love, not in the desire to be admired by others. I want to be loved for who I am. I want to love others for who they are. Please help me understand your truth and how the truth of who you are can change my heart. Thank you for loving me. Amen.

Chapter 2

What Are Optics?
Kind of a Big Deal

Glittering entertainers arrive at awards shows and strut down the red carpet. We hear announcers comment on their every thread. We watch them air-kiss people they probably won't be speaking to by the end of the evening. They have long since learned to do whatever it takes to keep up appearances. They play nice with "frenemies," dodge paparazzi who try to catch them unaware, hire stylists, spend long hours in the gym, and on and on it goes. As if the pressure to keep up an image is not intense enough already, some Hollywood elites took it to a new level, as in, one level down—to the next generation.

Fearing their privileged children wouldn't get into the "right" college or university, some wealthy entertainers a few years back invented a work-around. They simply paid to get their kids in. It's as if they wanted to see their kid still wearing the superhero cape from faded Halloween pictures, even if the child was anything but. The problem was, these parents got caught. Federal prosecutors charged dozens of people with bribing athletic coaches and cheating on entrance exams. Careers ended and heads rolled at some of the nation's most elite universities as one after another was found guilty. Famous people went to jail.[1]

Just another Hollywood scandal? Yes, and more than that. These actions were shocking because of what they revealed about the culture we live in. People want to be seen as the best of the best . . . even if they aren't . . . and they'll do whatever it takes to achieve that—*no matter whether it's legal or not.* The big deal about this scandal is that it allowed us to see and experience in real time *the shallowing of humanity.* This is a cultural shift that has taken place over the last 20 years. We used to believe that what's on the *inside* of a person is what matters. Now it seems we think that what's on the *outside* counts even more.

This focus on appearances is called *optics. Optics* is the word you've heard all over the media to describe how good or bad something appears.

Early in the evolution of our current obsession with optics, William Safire, who penned *The New York Times*'s "On Language" column, noted, "Optics is hot, rivaling content." The column's subhead read, "A scientific-sounding buzzword for 'public relations.'"[2] Over a decade ago, Safire saw that it was becoming more important to appear to be truthful than to actually *tell* the truth.

In other words, spin is everything. If what we have to say to our audience or platform isn't that great, we just give it a little twist and add a little shine. (Really, it's okay. No one will notice or care, right?) In the world of politics, people are *paid* to do that. They're called spin doctors, publicists, and marketing experts. They take the optics . . . and fabricate them, the way people used to tell a story— "spin a yarn"—in the old days, to make them seem better than they really are. The schedule of how and when these spinmeisters inform the press is referred to as the spin cycle. Spin is real and goes on every day. It's an *occupation*.

Spin has filtered through our culture. We don't just twist what we mean to make it sound better; we even take words and change their definitions. Whatever meaning we want to adopt becomes the new definition. *Bad* means good. *Tight* means cool. And *sick* means awesome.

Weird, but as you might have guessed, I have a theory as to why we love doing this.

First, did you know that the Oxford English Dictionary picks one word annually as their "word of the year"? It's true. One such pick—the one from 2016—sent chills up my spine. It not only foretold a trend of 2016 but also a trend for the decade. The word was *posttruth*. Here's how it's explained . . .

"Relating to or denoting circumstances in which objective facts are less influential in shaping public opinion than appeals to emotion and personal belief."

Allow me to offer *superoptics* as a candidate for 2021 word of the year. This takes the whole posttruth concept a scary step further. Having already demoted truth in favor of feelings, superoptics elevates the appearance or virtual perception of reality over reality itself.

Armed with an adequate understanding of the power of superoptics, trolls, political pundits, false religious leaders, spin doctors, and opinion news media can not only take the focus off of truth but can also bend it like the magicians in the "Mistborn" world. Author Brandon Sanderson called the magic in his wildly popular fantasy books Allomancy, Feruchemy, and Hemalurgy. All three magic systems are based on metals, which are used by the magician to grant them specific abilities. The magicians were called Mistings, Mistborn, and Twinborn. Modern-day spin doctors aren't as elaborate—they haven't even adopted a moniker, so let me do it for them.

I call the wielders of superoptics *truthbenders*, based on their most powerful ability—the super high-level, yoga-master bending of truth so thorough as to render it unrecognizable from actual facts.

Truthbenders are far more dangerous than their precursors— "truth-deflectors"—in that they create whole new realities that are characterized almost exclusively on being entirely made up.

Today we are living *not* in a posttruth culture but rather in a truth-altering, optics-twisting virtual reality, led by the next generation of spin doctors called truthbenders.

Okay, rant over. Now, back to my theory and why we love it. It's really what this book is all about.

Facts, reality, and truth are impartial, and as such, they can be brutal at times. In a world where optics trump all three, it seems like an acceptable compromise to many to bend the truth sometimes for the more comfortable purpose of presenting more favorable personal optics. We witness this on the news, political websites, and reading people's Instagram, Facebook, and Twitter rants. And we do this in pictures, text, and even in what we say in conversations.

It's not even that important if what you say is right . . . you just have to say it confidently. It's no longer the most skillful debater who wins a debate. It is the loudest, most dramatic, most confident. To win the debate, you don't have to be honest; you just have to know how to work the crowd. *Smile and wave, boys. Smile and wave.*

It doesn't matter if what you're saying is pathetic, as long as you are persuasive. Often, if you are able to put down the other person before they can put you down, you win. Prosecuting attorneys have long been stymied by defense attorneys who open their arguments with "Now, this prosecutor is going to try to tell you . . . " Then they lay out the prosecution's entire argument and start poking holes in it. There's nothing left for the prosecutor to say. The juries and Court TV fans get suckered into believing lies.

From Washington's spin doctors to courtroom dramatics to Hollywood's hip publicists, optics is less about truth and more about perception. How does the world see us? And does it like what it sees?

We learn how the world sees us pretty early in life. At least, I know I did. No one thought I was a superhero, that's for sure. All it took was a soul-crushing round of dodgeball to show me how they saw me. And that, in turn, informed how I saw myself.

The Optics of Dodgeball

I know of few games better designed to shred a kid's self-esteem than dodgeball. I mean, unless you are one of those rare ones who had muscles at 11 or, if you were a boy, could grow a full beard by age 12.

In case you have never had the joy—or heartache—of playing dodgeball, let me break it down for you. Two teams line up opposite each other, each with a number of rubber balls. The goal is to hit the members of the other team with the balls. If you are hit, you are out. The first team to get out every member of the other team wins. If this sounds fascinating, you can see it in action in the old Ben Stiller and Vince Vaughn film creatively named *Dodgeball.*

This game, I assume, was designed by psychotherapists to ensure people would eventually land on a therapist's couch. But the game's torment doesn't start with a rubber ball in the face. It begins way before you set foot on the court. Before a single ball is thrown, you go through a ritual more intense than anything the Navy Seals ever devised. I'm talking about "picking teams." This sadomasochistic ritual is intended to break down your soul. It's that torturous, humiliating period that seems to stretch for days, when everything goes into slow motion as you twist inside, break into a sweat, get nauseous, and try to concentrate on dragonflies or drag racers or something nice you heard someone say about you one time. During this period, every insecurity you have is put on display for one purpose and one purpose alone: to allow other kids to hone their skills at sarcasm.

First, captains are picked. If you have any flaws at all, you don't stand a chance at being a captain. The captains then handpick each team player. Have you ever read *Lord of the Flies*? It's a novel about civilized boys stranded without adult supervision who become very uncivilized, very fast. Just like in the book, the first picks in dodgeball are predictable, with the fastest and most popular kids getting chosen first, and the weak and nerdy kids, praying the earth will open up and swallow them, are chosen last.

I was first introduced to the game when I was about six years old. This was around the same time that my head started growing . . . without my body. By the time I turned seven, my head was huge. I was christened with the highly creative nickname of "Big Head Little Body." What's this got to do with dodgeball? Well, if you, or any part of you, were a big target, you didn't get picked. My head was freakishly big. I'm talking E.T. big. So, I was usually picked after the slowest or least popular kid in the class. Which, upon reflection, might have meant that I was the least popular. Even if the tiniest girl was a kindergartener who happened to wander into the lineup area, she'd get picked before me. When it came to my giant dome, the optics were grim.

Only later would I learn that dodgeball was great preparation for today's reality. That is, how the crowd perceives you matters more than who you really are.

For some of us, optics has less to do with the schoolyard and more to do with our home life. Often, it's those who are the closest to us—uncles, aunts, brothers, sisters, cousins, or parents—who have the hardest time believing we can be anything other than how they see us:

- baby of the family
- little brother
- punk kid
- spoiled brat
- runt of the litter

The people who know us best have a hard time believing there's anything special about us because they think they already know everything about us. They know where we've been and what we've done. They know our mistakes and our immaturity. It's the old "prophet is never welcomed in his hometown" proverb Jesus talked about in Luke 4:24.

The 1912 presidential race featured a three-candidate contest that captivated the world's attention. Woodrow Wilson defeated both Republican incumbent Howard Taft and former President Teddy Roosevelt, who broke from the Republicans and formed a third party. Wilson became the first Democrat president in 20 years and the first Southerner to hold the office since the Civil War. Wilson's presidency would encompass a world war and change world history. As Wilson tied up loose ends before his inauguration, he visited an aging aunt. In the course of their conversation, Aunt Janie said, "Well, what are you doing now?" He answered, "I've been elected president, Aunt Janie." She replied, "President of what?"

I love that story. Has something like that ever happened to you? The person Aunt Janie thinks you are will stick with her for life. Optics will always be with us. And so will the naysayers and the people who underestimate us. Every day of our lives, for the rest of our lives. (Super uplifting thought, right?) Optics is present in relationships, at school, in our workplaces. Social media just hypes it up even more.

> **"Today's message is clear: How you look and how you are perceived actually *determine* who you are."**

Today's message is clear: how you look and how you are perceived actually *determine* who you are.

Optics Overload

Advertisers know that "image is everything." For years, actors in white lab coats announced in cigarette ads that doctors endorsed smoking. It was decades before smokers who'd been duped into believing those advertising lies were able to sue, after some 130,000 people died each year from smoking-related causes. Believing an image can be deadly, and yet for a lot of people, "image is everything" remains true. Image seems more important than reality. Consider some areas where perception has replaced reality:

1. Appearing as if we're having a good day is more important than admitting when we need help.

2. Feelings are more important than facts.

3. Political correctness is more important, and believable, than truth.

4. Ideology is more important than history.

5. Spin is more important than accuracy.

6. Group identity is more important than who you actually are.

7. Readership is more important than correct reporting.

We have become a nation where the optics of *everything* trumps the reality of *anything*. In so many ways, our own feelings of self-worth are directly tied to the way others perceive us. No wonder we try so hard to "spin" our own lives.

The irony of our present use of optics is that it distorts the real meaning of "optics" that was established centuries ago. Optics was never about spin. Author Jeff Bairstow writes, "Newton and Galileo might well be appalled at the more contemporary uses of the word optics. . . . "[3] Because 400 years ago, *optics was all about revealing the truth*. Today it's far more popular to crowdsource truth.

> "We have become a nation where the optics of *everything* trumps the reality of *anything*."

Revealing the Truth

Originally, the word *optics* had nothing to do with perception or spin. It had to do with revealing *reality*. Optics is the science that studies the genesis and propagation of light. Galileo was one of the first astronomers to utilize optics. He built the first telescope, leading him to discover this truth about our galaxy that shocked the world: the earth is not the center of our solar system—the earth revolves around the sun. This might seem like Science 101 to you. *Of course the earth revolves around the sun.* But this revolutionary idea was viewed as heresy by church leaders of the time. And since the church was the head of the government, Galileo spent the rest of his life under house arrest.[4]

> ## "Truth does not change based on our ability to stomach it."
>
> —FLANNERY O'CONNOR

Sir Isaac Newton, born the same year that Galileo died, picked up where Galileo left off.[5] Newton's work in optics redefined how we look at light. You might remember him as the guy who sat under an apple tree and discovered gravity, but he did more than that. Newton found he had difficulty seeing clearly through the lens of a telescope. A rainbowlike halo of refracted light from the glass lens distorted the image. Newton replaced the lens with metal mirrors to create a reflective technology that showed images more clearly. His innovative breakthrough is still in use today. Today's Hubble telescope uses a cutting-edge version of Newton's reflective technology to reveal the truth about our galaxy and show that there are billions of galaxies yet to be explored.[6]

At its origin, optics was all about revealing the truth. Things have changed quite a bit in the last half a millennium. But one thing hasn't—truth itself. I like the way Flannery O'Connor put it, "Truth does not change based on our ability to stomach it."

What Are Your Optics?

Optics have been used to spin war results and gloss over character flaws. They've been used to hide mistakes and mask failures. They've even been used to change school textbooks and completely rewrite history. It sounds as if I'm blaming government and big business for those things. But I'm not. Read it again. This is how we *all* use optics today, for the everyday living of our own lives.

Social media loves optics. You may have never put up a truly spontaneous photo of yourself and your friends without checking several shots of the exact same thing first and getting everyone's approval on how they looked. You may have never tweeted your real feelings without couching it in political correctness. And you may have posted something only after it was edited, deleted, reposted, edited again . . . until finally you achieved your own stamp of approval—approving *yourself* for being *yourself.*

Why do we do these things to ourselves? For one thing, image *does* matter. In one of the first cases to be called "public shaming," communications executive Justine Sacco, a South African, tweeted short, clumsy jokes about the indignities of travel as she made her way home from the US to visit family. According to *The Guardian*, she "made a puerile tweet that linked Aids with race."[7] As she landed after her 11-hour trip, her phone blew up with messages. She discovered that far beyond reaching her 170 Twitter followers, her tweet had lit up the world with indignance, and now the top-trending hashtag worldwide was #HasJustineLandedYet.[8] As she slept on her flight, she lost her job and reputation and gained a new one, a bad one. On the other hand, just 10 years earlier, Paris Hilton had gone in the completely opposite direction, going from being seemingly nobody to somebody; after putting together trendy images of herself and occasional inane statements, she became one of the first people to be called "famous for being famous."

As we watch stories like these, we sometimes assume, or maybe we've been taught, that we should strive for errorless perfection ourselves. We don't want to come across as being "less than" or, even worse, forgettable. To get the kind of attention we long for, we shape how we reveal ourselves to the world. We may use only positive thoughts, positive confessions, and positive actions. I'm all in favor of positivity, but not when we're refusing to accept reality and just lying to ourselves.

The truth is, none of us is perfect. So why do we try to present ourselves that way? Admitting our weaknesses is not doubt or fear. It goes back to the original meaning of optics—seeing ourselves for who we really are.

Honesty sets us up for authentic relationships. Being genuine invites truth and clarity into our lives. Dishonesty does the opposite. When we pretend we are perfect, we deny our need for help. Instead of our transparency, our "weakness," becoming our strength, our faked "strength" becomes our weakness.

Perfection isn't a #goal . . . it's an #impossibility.

When we insist on building the illusion that we have life under control, all amazing and perfect, we barricade ourselves from getting the help we need.

Deep down, don't we all want what is real? And authentic? How long can we live with the spin? And how long before the optics wear off and the world sees you for *you*?

The Real You

Expectations placed on people have never been higher than today. For women, the expectation often focuses on appearance over accomplishment. In one recent 12-month period, YouTube logged 169 billion views just for beauty-related content alone.[9]

This culture of expectation and perfection prompted singer-songwriter Colbie Caillat to release *Try*, an anthem about authenticity. The thought-provoking song poked holes in the optics of fashion and the unrealistic expectations placed on women. In her lyrics, Caillat invited women to reveal their true selves by taking their makeup off, letting their hair down, and embracing their natural beauty. It was an anti-super-you anthem.

To answer her own lyrics, Caillat started her music video in full makeup and, verse by verse, shed the optics. Off came her hair extensions. Then her fake eyelashes. Then the truckloads of eyeliner, shadow, and mascara. By the song's end, stripped down to her natural beauty, she basically asks the listener, *Do you like yourself?* It can be a hard question to answer.

The same year Caillat's song came out, an Australian newscaster named Karl Stefanovic became frustrated by the unsolicited advice viewers offered his female counterpart, Lisa Wilkinson, about her clothing.[10] He did a social experiment by wearing the same suit every day for a year. At the end, according to him, "Nobody said a thing." The optics for him were different than for her. Within a year, female newscasters and movie and music stars across the US were having their photos taken, or doing entire television shows, without makeup, just to make the same statement.

Now, let's be honest, even without hair extensions and lip gloss, most thought Colbie Caillat still looked amazing, as did Alicia Keys, Kim Kardashian, and many of the women who allowed themselves to appear without makeup. My guess? That they still chose the best "makeup-free" pics out of the seven billion they took. And let's also be honest: all of these people went back to wearing makeup, and newscaster Karl, who stood up for women, went back to changing his suit each day. But they all made a big point. Optics *isn't* everything—or shouldn't be.

Do you like yourself? Good question. It seems we are buying in to optics, heart and soul, not just because we're not sure if the world likes us but because . . . *we are not sure we even like ourselves.*

For most of us, when we think of ourselves without our self-made optics, all we see is "Big Head Little Body." When we look at our shortcomings and mistakes, we tend to resign ourselves to where we are. Our thoughts and beliefs about ourselves reveal our secret fears. What our family members said on their worst day—and probably didn't even mean—lingers. *I'll never succeed. My best efforts are too little, too late. I can never be enough on my own. There is no hope.*

As a result, we'd rather have the fake optics than the harsh reality of what we feel about ourselves. We buy in to the promise of optics because our messed-up lives and the truth of how we really feel about ourselves hurts too much. We know our own failures and inadequacies. We want others to have a better perception of us than we have of ourselves.

Too often we take stock of our *own* negative words and give up in despair. We think our problems are painfully apparent and our failures are agonizingly obvious. We feel they'll keep us from the authentic relationships and life-giving connections we are longing for.

As a result, we file our dreams under "fairy tales." We are who we are, the worst of what we tell ourselves, and we fear nothing can change that. Yet deep in our souls we are hoping beyond hope . . . for hope.

So, what do we do with our weaknesses? How do we react to the fact that we are flawed, and our flaws seem to be disqualifying us from our dreams? In our next chapter, I will introduce you to a freeing principle called *Opposite Day*.

A CHANGE OF HEART

We have become a nation where the optics of *everything* trumps the reality of *anything.*

THINK

- Optics is less about truth and more about perception. It describes how good or bad something appears, rather than its reality.

- We use optics in our own lives so that others will like us better than we like ourselves.

- We'd rather have fake optics than the harsh reality of how we feel about our problems, our failures, and ourselves.

- During the times of Newton and Galileo, optics had to do with revealing reality.

- When we pretend we are perfect, we deny our need for help. Honesty with ourselves and others sets us up for authentic relationships.

PAUSE

- People want to be seen as the best of the best . . . even if we aren't . . . no matter what. How do you agree or disagree with this statement in your own life?

- What is a "dodgeball" or "Big Head Little Body" moment that has defined how you see yourself?

- Do you like the "real" you? Why or why not?

- What would it feel like to be honest with yourself and others about who you are instead of relying on spin or optics?

CONNECT

The Lord is close to all who call on him, yes, to all who call on him in truth. (Psalm 145:18, NLT)

Search me, O God, and know my heart; test me and know my anxious thoughts. (Psalm 139:23, NLT)

RESPOND

God, I want to learn how to be honest with myself and with those I love. Teach me how to anchor my life in your truth, not in others' perceptions of me. You know me inside and out. The good, the bad, and the ugly. You know that I am not perfect and never will be. I give all my anxiety, my failures, and my struggles to you. You have promised to be close to me. Reveal your truth and hope in my life. Thank you for loving me, imperfections and all. Amen.

Chapter 3

Optics and Opposite Day

Thirteen months before I was born, my mother gave birth to twins—one boy, one girl. We were all so close in age that Mom basically had triplets on her hands. It was my older brother, Mike the twin, who competed with me for almost everything.

During my "Big Head Little Body" years, it never occurred to Mike to have some mercy on his kid brother who was struggling. Instead, he made sure I lost at everything. And by everything, I mean every competition, every fight, every race, every game that Mike and I ever played. Actually, there was no competition at all. My brother was the victor. Then, one day, my torso caught up with my head, and my body was in balance. That's when I discovered an intoxicating fact—I could *win*. Or, at the very least, in anything and everything, I could be a legitimate competitor. Now it was time for revenge. All I wanted to do was take Mike down. I wanted to be the best for a change.

This drove my mom crazy. We would compete in sports, drama, grades, comedy, who could get the parents to give in first, who could get from the car to the front door first, who could drink a glass of milk the fastest . . . *everything*. And it didn't stop there. If my mom even *tried* to get us to consider the merits of the other person, we weren't having it. For instance, she'd say something like, "Hey, Mike, don't you think your brother sounds good singing?" Mike's automatic reply would be "Yeah, if it's opposite day."

Opposite day. Remember saying this as a kid? It was the ultimate trump card after "I know you are, but what am I?" Saying it was "opposite day" was a clever way to turn everything on its head and become the champion of whatever was being discussed.

"You are super popular . . . if it's opposite day."

"I love your hair . . . if it's opposite day."

"That joke you just told is my favorite ever . . . if it's opposite day."

Now, here's a life-altering suggestion for you. If you want to embrace who you really are, if you are longing for authentic relationships and true life-giving connections, have an "opposite day" on the optics.

Beyond the Optics

What does "opposite day" with the optics look like? Living by optics teaches us to grab any self-promoting event or circumstance and squeeze it for everything it's worth. Andy Warhol famously coined the phrase "15 minutes of fame," and it seems some people are intent on making sure they get theirs. We want to put all our eggs in the optics basket. Living by optics says our value comes from how others perceive us.

If our value is tethered to what we display on the outside—looks, displays of wealth, intelligence, passion, political savvy, humor, power—where anything we feel is measured externally, we can turn that idea on its head.

Optics is the opposite of *authenticity*.

We can take *optics* back to its original meaning. Galileo and Newton had it right. We need the truth . . . not a distortion of what is real. We need clarity about the value of life and who we are to find out what our true purpose is.

We need an optical revelation . . . and a truth revolution.

Authentic You

Like Colbie Caillat's song says, you don't have to give away the truth of who you are just to appease the crowds. Your "super you" won't set you free. If anything, that burden of trying to be perfect will only break you down.

Your honesty, with yourself and with the world, is what unleashes the hope that you are longing for. There is another way to live your life and look at the world. There is more for you than people-pleasing optics. (Those people were never really that pleased anyway . . .)

When you anchor yourself in authenticity, you get to change your view of what really matters. Image is *not* everything. Not even close.

> "When you anchor yourself in authenticity, you get to change your view of what really matters."

Your value isn't measured by what you look like or how you are perceived. Living in "opposite day" reveals that your worth is, in reality, measured by the depth of your character and the desires of your heart.

Optics crush the soul; authenticity frees the soul. Optics kill, authenticity brings life. Choosing between the two is not just a casual choice, because it's bedrock to who you are and what you will live for. The question is . . . which will you choose?

Learn from the Past

For a moment, just think of it. Newton and Galileo were not the people who *invented* optics. They were just the ones in modern history who *identified* and *defined* it. As much as we'd like to believe "things were better way back when," the truth is, people have always been the same—just *people*. All the complaints about how bad the government is? Go grab that US history textbook you used to fall asleep reading. Government has been messy since the nation began. All the ways movie stars obsess about wanting their name everywhere—even to the point of putting it on a star on the sidewalk of a dirty street in Hollywood? Yeah, that obsession has been around since time began. And the dictators who put their image everywhere? Yes, it's all been done as far back as you can go.

Ask a fan of ancient history, or an archaeologist, or just google it—when ancient civilizations are dug up, what we find are coins with the image or name of a leader. When we unearth a pyramid or discover ancient caves, we find drawings and graffiti and statues and pottery shards and jewelry and money, and on just about anything that was created by people, we find images, self-likenesses, and people's names. Perhaps it's the artist's image or the leader's name. What's so new about all this today?

#Selfitis

Humanity's love of optics coupled with today's love of social media has led to the identification of a new "disease" that is almost a pandemic. If you haven't been infected, you know someone who has. It isn't the flu. Or even the common cold. It is . . . selfitis. Selfitis is the obsessive taking of selfies.[1]

While personal photos used to feature landscapes, group shots, and family events, more and more, we are seeing singular photos focused on a single person . . . taken by that same person. *Selfitis* isn't a diagnosis that's been added to the medical books. The term was coined because something needed to describe the condition of over-the-top selfie taking. And that habit, or obsession, is no joke. Selfitis is a growing concern that is being researched by psychologists and journalists alike. Dr. Janarthanan Balakrishnan and Dr. Mark D. Griffiths have identified the following psychological factors behind the spread of selfitis:[2]

• the need to boost self-confidence

• competitiveness to see who can get more likes (#winning)

• the need to get others to pay attention to you

• the desire to alter your mood and make yourself feel better

• the need to fit in with your social group

Get this: as a global community, we upload 1.8 billion digital images a day.[3] So. Many. Selfies. Selfies can be a whole lot of fun. And who doesn't love a good photobomb? But while they can be an important form of self-expression, selfies can also promote that anxiety-ridden "super you" mentality.

The filtered, photoshopped, and cropped versions of our-selves that we share via our edited selfies can be detrimental to our psychological well-being. Studies show a direct link between altered photos and narcissism. Which seems like a pretty easy connection to make. Is there a more narcissistic word than *selfie*? Probably not.

The Ever-Popular Notion of Narcissism

Most preteens today know the popular word *narcissism*, which means excessive self-absorption.[4] Basically, it is used when people become the center of their own universe and are obsessed with themselves. The selfie is an example of narcissism at work. While taking a selfie, we are usually positioned forward in the frame, larger than life, and those we pose with (if we actually pose with other people) are diminished in the background. We heart us a whole lot.

Narcissism isn't just an adolescent issue. It is a human condition that transcends age, race, gender, or financial status. Your average two-year-old has it on lock. As evidenced in those cave drawings, it has been around since pretty much the beginning of time. We all like to think that the sun rises and sets . . . on us. To become well-rounded, loving humans, we have to battle those natural self-centered tendencies.

Battling our own self-centered nature is hard stuff, but it has to be done. A narcissistic lifestyle is ultimately destructive to us and the people we care about. Have you ever been around someone who is completely self-absorbed? Didn't ya love it?! Of course not—it's like having "Nails on a Chalkboard" on repeat on Spotify. Being a narcissist means we don't show a whole lot of concern for anyone other than ourselves, so it is directly at odds with our hopes for authentic relationship.

We can see narcissism at work in the news across the globe daily. The more status we have, the easier it is to succumb. Movie stars, recording artists, business moguls, celebrities, politicians, and professional athletes are especially susceptible to its pull. Heads of government have a hard time separating their influential jobs from their own self-importance. With that much power, it is easy for someone to think they are the most important person in the galaxy. And so, they run for president. Or leave the group to cut a solo album. Or launch a clothing line. Or change their name to an unpronounceable symbol. Who wants to listen to or wear *that*?

Caution: As we take this journey together, there will be caution signs along the way whenever we need to navigate through a statement with extra care. The paragraph you just read was one such place. Though it may not bear saying because of the guard rails, there is a drop-off we don't want to get cocky about. Obviously there is a certain amount of confidence and trust in ability we all need to possess if we're ever going to venture out and take on bigger and bigger things. But there is an important difference between confidence and conceit—between ability and arrogance. Just as there is an important distinction between following God and thinking we are God. When we insert ourselves in the place of God, we are in essence repeating the world's oldest sin. I'm talking about when the serpent in the garden of Eden convinced Adam and Eve that they would do better *playing* God than God Almighty does at actually *being* God. Theirs may have been the first time we saw this sinful pride employed, but it was far from the last.

Let's go back to the bad choice made by that ancient civilization. From their example, we can get perspective on what to do—and what not to do. It involves a good-looking king in ancient Israel who found out the hard way that narcissism can bring all your dreams to a grinding halt and cause you to self-destruct. Obsessing about yourself has a way of doing that.

And from whose viewpoint do we learn this? Ancient scholars. The writings of prophets, or "seers" in Israel, record their tight connection to God. Yes, through their writings, we find out how God, the one who breathed life into humans in the first place, views the optics of the people he created.

Meet King Saul

An ancient group of people made a really bad choice and suffered as a nation because of it. What was their mistake way back then? Optics. You likely have heard of the 10 plagues of Egypt, Moses crossing the Red Sea, Joshua "fighting" the battle of Jericho, or the pyramids in Egypt, which may have been built by Jewish slaves. At the very least, you know about modern Israel—that tiny, fierce nation over in the Middle East.

Modern Israel can trace its roots back to the small but mighty nation that got its start when Moses led the Hebrew nation out of slavery in Egypt. A loving, perfect God sent Moses to get them out of there, then helped and protected them as they traveled up to what is now present-day Israel.[5] God's loving commands, his "10 commandments," shaped their beliefs and actions. And the Israelites loved him back—or mostly tried to love him. (There are always a few bad apples.) As for an acting government, God handpicked prophets and governors called *judges* who followed him and heard his voice.

And there was a cycle the people fell into during these times that remains with them (and most of humanity) to this day. It was the cycle of taking for granted much of the blessing and favor in our lives during times of plenty and crying out for that same blessing and favor once it's removed and we enter times of hardship and need. Some might point to this and say, "That's just human nature," but it's more than that. It's a cycle that the Lord warned his people about over and over and over and over and . . . (insert several hundred more *overs* here) again. But despite these warnings voiced through the many prophets and judges that God sent, most of the Israelites preferred to learn lessons via a two-by-four in the middle of the forehead. And so do we.

Here's exactly how the cycle went:

Step 1, **Disengagement.** The people would stop daily worship and disengage with God, preferring to engage secular culture and the false gods and customs of the nations around them (Judges 2:10).

Step 2, **Disobedience.** Now the people no longer see the value (read here, "fun") in obeying God and his ways—so they rebel (Judges 2:11).

Step 3, **Desertion.** Here, the people don't even pretend to worship God. Instead, they desert the Almighty for the false gods of other nations to serve them (Judges 2:11–12).

Step 4, **Distress.** Whenever the Israelites tried to take matters into their own hands, calamity was the result (Judges 2:15).

Step 5, **Discipline.** God uses their enemies to teach them about the consequences of their sin and disobedience (Judges 2:15).

Step 6, **Desperation.** The hardship and oppression get so bad that in desperation, the people cry out to God for help (Judges 2:15).

Step 7, **Deliverance.** God raises up judges to lead his people out of the time of discipline and back into his sovereign will (Judges 2:16).

FORK IN THE ROAD

At this point the people either listen to what God is telling them through the judges (and return to a time of God's blessing and favor), or they dig in deeper and move back to step 2 . . .

wash,

rinse,

repeat.

Why do I include all of this? Because this ancient cycle *hasn't changed one bit* in thousands of years! We've seen this cycle in America dozens of times, and we are in the middle of it as I write this. And if we ever want to see God's favor and blessing again, like Israel, we must repent and return to the Lord. The exact things the Lord looked for then he still looks for today. It's spelled out very clearly in 2 Chronicles 7:14, "If my people who are called by my name will humble themselves, and pray and seek my face, and turn from their wicked ways, then I will hear from heaven, and will forgive their sin and heal their land."

Let me break it down.

- **My people**—Christians

- **Called by my name**—serious Christ followers

- **Humble themselves**—stop playing God

- **Pray**—engage God again

- **Seek my face**—not empty religion, but a real and vital relationship with Christ

- **Turn from their wicked ways**—a complete 180

- **THEN**—and not until then

- **I will hear from heaven**—reengage them

- **Forgive**—restore the broken fellowship

- **Heal their land**—favor and blessing

This system, or at least some form of it, is how the fledgling nation got its start, and it's what led the people of Israel for their first 430 years. But things changed.

Even after hundreds of years of this obvious-to-a-kindergartener cycle, the people weren't learning. In fact, they managed to blame God and every judge he sent. So God allowed them to enter another season.

Israel started losing battles as a result of disobeying God, but they wouldn't accept the responsibility for it. Instead, they blamed it on someone or something else—the leaders, God, their neighbors, conservatives, climate change—whoever. Okay, I threw those last two in to keep you on your toes. Then, some political leaders would stoke the people's discomfort until the entire nation of Israel went into a flat-out insurrection.

Just imagine Israel as an NFL team. After years of ongoing battles and wars, Israel wrapped up another losing season against its enemies. The Philistine nation was the current opposing team that kept whipping them. But Israel was tired of coming in last place. The people wanted a winning streak. They were tired of being ruled by coaches who followed a God-centered playbook. In their discontent, they decided that the coach, if not the whole playbook, had to go—it wasn't winning.

Finally, during a time when the judge-turned-prophet was a man named Samuel, Israel had had enough. As a nation, they announced they were sick of Coach Samuel. They wanted a new coach—one that would make them more like the hipper, cooler teams around them. There were no presidents or prime ministers during this period of history. And there were certainly no judges ruling any other countries.[6] Leadership was all about *kings*. Israel didn't want just a mere coach. Of course not! They wanted a *king*.

The problem was that in their whining about the theocracy—the coach and playbook handed down from God—the people of Israel were showing their change of heart. It wasn't Samuel that Israel was rejecting but God himself. What the people were saying was that they just didn't want to be ruled by God anymore. God would have to be benched.

God knew that being ruled by kings wasn't all unicorns and rainbows like Israel thought it was going to be. He knew that when there's a king, people give up certain rights. God had given them a righteous government where they could petition judges and seek justice. But Israel wasn't having it.

So, God gave Israel what they wanted, not because they were right or because they convinced him to change his mind but because sometimes the best lessons learned are the hardest (back to the two-by-four). He told Samuel to let Israel have a king, and the nation went wild. They took the first-round draft pick without even consulting God. They wanted a Heisman Trophy winner, someone who would help them kick butt in battle. Their first choice was the tallest and most handsome man in the nation. And they got him. They got Saul. Saul![7] There was even a scouting report on Saul. It said, "Saul was the most handsome man in Israel—head and shoulders taller than anyone else in the land."[8]

What? They went for . . . *looks*? You can't make this stuff up. It doesn't sound as if they're picking a king. It sounds as if Israel picked someone for the cover of *GQ*, or nominated him for the *People* magazine issue of Handsomest Man Alive. Apparently, Saul was a Brad-Pitt-Chris-Hemsworth-John-Legend look-alike who also had LeBron-like skills on the basketball court. Just the kind of guy you want to run a whole country. So, the prophet Samuel went with it. He anointed Saul the first king of Israel.

Saul had everything going for him in terms of optics. He was literally head and shoulders taller than every man in Israel and had a reputation for being incredibly good-looking. He had the kind of handsome that never had to wait for a table. As a warrior, he recruited people, built an army, and led his men to victory after victory. The people sang songs about his victories. As a king, Saul built things and got stuff done. As a result, the nation loved him. They listened to him. By today's standards, he'd have a 99 percent approval rating. He was a king, their king, and everybody was happy . . . for a while.

Saul, like so many people who gain fame, became the victim of his own press. He believed the optics about himself. He started trusting what people, external sources, said about him. He believed the songs people sang about him. He was reactive, listening to the outside instead of having a good heart on the inside. Saul's character was lacking. He was a poser through and through. Saul never matured beyond being the center of his own universe.

Saul's pride and confidence in his own abilities led to an unwillingness to do what God wanted, or even what was good for the nation. There came a point when Saul didn't want to wait around for God to call the next play, regardless of what it meant to the team. He was more interested in optics than substance. After all, he figured, he couldn't just sit around *waiting*. What would people think? He was the *king*.

He had plays of his own, so he decided to call an audible. As a result, he flat-out disobeyed what God told him to do. Specifically, he was supposed to wait for Samuel to pray, but when Samuel delayed his arrival, Saul took on the role of the prophet. Wrong. Not his job. Saul lost God's favor and Israel's trust.[9] The scribes described his unraveling in eight words that no one ever wants to have written about them: "The Spirit of the Lord departed from Saul."[10]

But it's a bit of a leap from self-absorbed to making yourself a spiritual figurehead and taking on the role of worship leader for the sacrifice. How did this happen?

Well, not as randomly as we might think. You see, Saul had been setting himself up as the all-encompassing supreme, Kim Jong-un of all of Israel—even above God. It started with a selfitis mentality, grew into full-blown selfitis, and eventually saw him setting up all things of worship to point to himself over God. He didn't start out that way, but he certainly ended up that way—and, if we're not careful, we can too.

How?

Well, while most of us don't start out filing a 501(c)(3) for our Facebook account and setting it up as an official church, we might be surprised at how many end up there.

No, when we start a Facebook, Twitter, or Instagram account, we just want to (as I said earlier) reconnect with people and be in the know. But some don't know how to leave it at that—King Saul certainly didn't, and that's why it was an easy step from being king to acting prophet and even receiver of godlike worship.

Now, before we get all down on Saul, keep in mind that plenty of people are doing this same thing today. It just looks different. One more time, first, we set up social media accounts to make friends or to reconnect with people—but soon find all the praise in the forms of comments, likes, and heart emojis to be quite a rush. So we tweak our avatars and bios to look even better so that we can garner even more of these powerful little dopamine hits that come in the form of tiny thumbs-ups. And before we know it, some of us have set up Facebook as a mini worship center to ourselves.

Think about it. We receive worship in the form of compliments and praise. We receive validation through how many people like our page. Eventually, we might even go over the 5K limit for a regular page and have to convert to a fan page to keep on growing.

A what page? A "*fan*" page. Gone are the purposes of community and encouragement—now we simply let our "fans" take care of the sacrifices of praise and worship while we bask in the glory.

Caution: Clarity is vital here. Perhaps you recall me saying at the beginning of this book that I'm not down on technology or social media—they're basically neutral, just like money. But both money and social media can be misused. And the line we cross from innocence to manipulation isn't all that clear. Perhaps that's why one of the most misquoted scriptures in all the Bible has to do with this very blurred line I'm referring to. Here's a test to show you what I'm talking about . . .

Have you ever heard the verse 1 Timothy 6:10? If so, I'll bet you remember it as follows: "Money is the root of all evil." That's not the entire verse, just the part most quoted, or perhaps I should say, most *mis*quoted. Here's the actual verse: "For the **love** of money is a **root** of **all kinds** of evil. Some people, eager for money, have wandered from the faith and pierced themselves with many griefs" (emphasis added). Kind of changes things, doesn't it? As I said, money is neutral. It's the **love** of money that leads to "all kinds of evil." That's bad enough. It hardly needs the reinforcing "all" in front of evil, but it's important to note that it's not "all" evil because there is something that comes before even the damaging worship of money.

Pride

Pride is the real precursor to destruction (Proverbs 16:18, "Pride goes before destruction, and a haughty spirit before stumbling")—including the love and worship of money (i.e., materialism). And pride is also the beginning of worshipping "likes," putting out fake avatars, and living off the desperation for approval that this book is all about. And once again, it's **not new**—social media is just the latest wrapping paper for it. As we've already seen, King Saul struggled greatly with pride and people pleasing.

Have you ever heard the old saying "Elvis has left the building"? Yep. Ever heard that "God is everywhere"? Yeah. Except with Saul. Saul rejected God through his own foolishness and pride. Dumb.

In a nation that was supposed to be God-centric, the message was pretty clear. God was letting Saul have his way . . . and Saul's way was a life without God. When the "Spirit of the Lord" left Saul, his days as Israel's play caller and self-appointed coach were numbered. Saul didn't have what it took to lead his nation. Soon, Israel needed a new king.

Making Picks

The NFL may not know much about kings, but it knows a whole lot about draft picks. There is one day that all teams, players, and coaches look forward to, and fans stay home from work to watch it on television. It's the NFL Draft.

On draft day, everyone pins their hopes for the next season to reshape teams with great players. Every die-hard fan is hoping their team gets the right player to turn their team around. And of course, there's that whole fantasy football thing, too.

Getting picked first is a huge honor for a player. Well, almost always a huge honor. It can be a huge embarrassment when the player's abilities don't end up translating into success in the big league. NFL history is littered with first-round draft picks that have floundered or flat-out failed. But it's still prestigious to be in *the first round*. After picking the first round, teams go to rounds two, three, four, five . . . Players generally have friends and family with them, waiting to celebrate. By the fourth round, people are getting embarrassed for the athlete. There simply is not a lot to brag about when you're a sixth-round pick. And if you're a quarterback and get chosen as the 199th pick overall, you'll be hoping they'll let you just smell the football, never mind touching it. The optics aren't great.

But optics don't have to define who you are. Your potential isn't determined by how others see you or what they say about you. Just ask Tom. Tom holds over 16 records in the NFL, including most times as Super Bowl MVP. He has 17 division titles. He has gone to the Super Bowl nine times in a 20-year career with the Patriots and has won six of those.[11] Tom Brady's career illustrates that being a sixth-round pick doesn't mean you're not a first-class player.[12] Optics are not always reality. There's life beyond the optics, as Tom Brady found out, and as Israel and Samuel soon found out with Saul.

> **"Optics are not always reality. There's life beyond the optics."**

Draft Day for Israel

For Israel, Saul was their first-round draft pick as king. His image looked good. But when it came to actually leading Israel in a right path and honoring the team owner (God), Saul was a bust. Israel had used optics to pick their king, choosing all flash and no substance. He followed his own lead. Bad choice. Eventually, he was cut from the team.

Israel had looked for a king with good optics. But God wanted something different. The good news is, Israel left him a pick. Bad news? It was the very last pick in the draft. No problem—the one God had in mind would turn out like Tom Brady, the best of the best. As it happened, God went looking for pretty much the polar opposite of what Israel had looked for. God gave Samuel specific instructions: "Do not look on his appearance or on the height of his stature, because I have rejected him. For the Lord sees not as man [humankind] sees, man [humankind] looks on the outward appearance, but the Lord looks on the heart."[13]

Perhaps God was teaching Israel that there was something more important than photoshopped pictures, fake profiles, doctored résumés, superhero avatars, self-promoting spin, sizzle reels, "friends" you don't know and will never meet, and faked perfection . . . Perhaps God was teaching Israel there's such a thing as *authenticity.*

God was definitely saying that we look at the optics, but *he looks beyond the optics.* God looks at the *heart.* An entire nation's future came down to the issue of optics. The truth that solved their problem will solve our dilemmas today.

The prophet Samuel didn't get it at first. But he was about to find out that God could not have cared less about skill set and good looks when it came to choosing a leader for his nation. God knew the person that he wanted for the job had to be a man with *heart.* God was very specific. He told Samuel the exact family to visit. He said (my paraphrase), "I want you to go near to the area of Bethlehem. There's a family there, and the father's name is Jesse. He has eight sons."

When Samuel arrived, Jesse's sons might not have known what was going on, but Jesse did. Samuel was a scout looking for a draft pick to be the next king. Jesse lined up his sons, starting with the oldest, Eliab. He was kind of a stud. He was tall (like Saul), and he was good-looking (like Saul). Samuel was elated. He sat waiting for the Spirit of the Lord to tell him if this was the one. He was probably thinking, *This is it! We're getting it on the first try. There can't be a better guy.*

You know Eliab was thinking the same thing: *"Yes, I'm all that!"*

Samuel was looking at the optics, but God said to Samuel's heart, *No, I haven't picked him. He's not the one.*

God wasn't looking at scouting reports, stats, the guy's muscles, or his jawline. Man looks at outside optics, but the Lord looks at the heart. Samuel rejected Eliab and each brother after that, making it through each round of Jesse's sons. The draft was over. There were no walk-ons. There were no free agents. And there was no king. The show was over. There was no one left to choose. Thanks for coming! Maybe next year.

Samuel intervened. "Wait, stop rolling the credits!" He asked Jesse, "Are these your only sons?"

No. Jesse had left one of his sons out of the lineup. "Well, there's the youngest, David, who's out tending the sheep," Jesse answered. Jesse didn't even think to include the redheaded boy who was watching the sheep out in the field. How is that for bad optics? Jesse must have thought his youngest son, David, was a "Big Head Little Body" guy. Perhaps David was the original redheaded stepchild. Maybe the son of an affair that Jesse had tried to keep secret. Whatever it was, Jesse figured David had no possible chance of being chosen by God. (This gives me so much hope.)

Even Samuel was tricked by the optics. He was about to make

a big mistake until he was gut-checked by God that there had to be another son. Samuel told Jesse he'd wait while Jesse sent for David. David arrived with no clue what was going on. He was probably all of 13 years old. His brothers were full-grown men. Samuel looked past every good-looking, tall brother and stopped at David. Then he did something remarkable. Samuel poured oil all over David's head,[14] a symbol that David was God's pick.[15]

In Jewish tradition, it is thought that Samuel leaned in and whispered to David, "This is the anointing oil of God, who has chosen you to be the next king of Israel."

The Founder of Opposite Day

What does God have to do with self-image, self-worth, authentic relationships, or how we plan our lives? God is the originator of Opposite Day. God is the only being who knows our deepest desires and our innermost thoughts. God is the only one who loves every bit of us, right down to our core. God is the one who, regardless of anything we say or do, says, "I choose you." "I *like* you." "You are important to me." And God is the *only* one who can take any ridiculously impossible situation we find ourselves in and turn it around in one minute.

What day was it when David was chosen to be king? Opposite Day. Now God called an audible. In football, an audible is called when the team breaks out of the huddle and comes to the line of scrimmage, and the quarterback observes that the defense has already figured out what the offense is going to do. So, the quarterback switches everything (calls an audible). An audible can be anything—but it's almost certainly going to be the opposite of what the defense was expecting. God called an audible—he did what was least expected by turning the last into the first, the bottom into the top, the youngest into the eldest who would rule over all.

Why did God choose David? Why would he skip over all those first-round draft picks and settle on "Big Head Little Body"? God looked at David's *heart*. He *knew* David's heart. David wasn't a narcissist. He didn't have selfitis. He wasn't obsessed with "all things David." He wasn't the center of his own universe.

God has a beautifully stealthy, almost sneaky way of doing the opposite of what we expect and of what we deserve. His values and priorities are just different from ours. His thoughts are higher than ours.

When I figured this out, it completely changed my world. God didn't judge me as a "Big Head Little Body" player. He made me feel valued. I remember every detail of the day that I realized he was choosing me to do something for him. Not because I was all that . . . but because he loved me. And I remember how God made me feel like his adopted child. He made me feel like a first-round draft pick.

God looks beyond the optics. The same God who chose David to be king and who put me on a specific life path is choosing you, too. When

> "God has a beautifully stealthy, almost sneaky way of doing the opposite of what we expect and of what we deserve."

you connect with God, crazy things start to happen. You stop self-destructing. You shed that "super you" image and start becoming the *authentic* you that you were meant to be.

God goes all Opposite Day on your life. When you give him your failures, he begins to prepare you for your greatest success.

When you fall flat on your face, he uses that failure to reshape your life. You thought you were disqualified. Perhaps you did something stupid that seemed life-shattering, or perhaps through no fault of your own, you were just having a "Big Head Little Body" season. And God is saying, "Nope. Doesn't matter. *I choose you.*"

How beautiful is that?! You were chosen by God! Let that sink in. And if that's not enough, add this: Psalm 139:1–4 and 13–16,

"O Lord, you have examined my heart and know everything about me. You know when I sit down or stand up. You know my thoughts even when I'm far away. You see me when I travel and when I rest at home. You know everything I do. You know what I am going to say even before I say it, Lord. . . . You made all the delicate, inner parts of my body and knit me together in my mother's womb. Thank you for making me so wonderfully complex! Your workmanship is marvelous—how well I know it. You watched me as I was being formed in utter seclusion, as I was woven together in the dark of the womb. You saw me before I was born. Every day of my life was recorded in your book. Every moment was laid out before a single day had passed."

God didn't wait for you to prove yourself before choosing you—he knew you and loved you before you were even born! That's how God rolls. And that's how he wants his representatives to roll, too.

What the team captain (Samuel) did that day was probably a marker moment for young David. Samuel essentially flipped the dodgeball script and went right for the "Big Head Little Body" player. And in doing so, he undoubtedly caused David to stand a little straighter, allowed him to lift his chin a little higher, and made his heart grow even stronger.

Contrast this with his family, who had trouble that same day even remembering their son and younger brother existed! I wonder how many times they demeaned him verbally with things like "What are you doing here, sheep boy?" or "Let the men handle this—your friends are out yonder in the pasture . . . run along, sheep boy." Some of it's recorded. I get into it when talking about a later stage of David's life—but there's no doubt in my mind that word wars start early in a family and get worse if they aren't snuffed out quickly.

Like it or not, words assign value—especially in the formative years—up or down. Constantly criticize a child, and their self-esteem will crater, usually bottoming out before they exit their teens. But when parents use words to edify instead, their children's self esteem begins to soar, carrying them throughout adulthood.

The Bible teaches us that every single man, woman, and child is highly valued by their heavenly Father. According to Genesis 1:26, we are created in his image. That image may be marred due to sin, but John 3:16 tells us God *still* loves us very much. How much? The Message paraphrase says it plainly: "This is how much God loved the world: He gave his Son, his one and only Son. And this is why: so that no one need be destroyed; by believing in him, anyone can have a whole and lasting life." He sent his Son on a rescue mission to purchase your freedom! I'd say that makes you priceless in the eyes of God! That's a biblical fact—but optics can make this impossible for some to see.

When I was a little boy and people called me "Big Head Little Body," it hurt. These unkind words created a powerful image during my most formative years, but do you know what would have hurt worse? If, after talking nice to me in a polite/politically correct and polished kind of way, I turned to leave, and they whipped out a baseball bat and actually bashed my head in.

Too much?

I agree, but we need to be honest—our society does it all the time. We react with outrage (usually fake) about the most juvenile tweets, careless Instagram posts, or Facebook rants as though the authors committed an unpardonable sin, but often we ignore truly horrific things happening on an epic scale and in shocking numbers like . . . wait for it.

Abortion.

How did this practice ever find its way into the rather sterile and harmless category of "health care"?

Simple—optics.

Those sarcastic little kids in second grade said some mean things, but kids will be kids—there was never a threat applied to their condescending words. Now, if an adult came along, heard the name calling, and added, "Yeah, and freaks like him don't deserve to live!"—well, that's a bit different. Their age and implied maturity, along with the stated threat just upped the optics ante, and a shift has occurred. If it goes no further, I would count myself lucky. But if some of the kids began associating this "Big Head Little Body" individual as detestable and problematic and took up sticks and stones as a result of the violence-endorsing words of the adult . . . well, all bets are off—like I said, a shift has occurred. Words that push the optics down a violent path *can* sometimes lead to physical harm.

How did we shift what I believe to be a gruesome procedure into politically correct, thoughtful, human-rights optics? Are we really no longer noticing that it's *not* very good for the health of the unborn child?

Again, optics.

Let's see how I think this has been done regarding abortion.

Before the 1960s, out-of-wedlock pregnancies placed quite

the stigma on women who found themselves in this difficult position. They were often looked down upon, whispered about, and
sometimes scorned altogether. Carefully crafted societal optics said
that these women were morally compromised. And many of these
women probably felt like the invisible and optical equivalent of a
scarlet letter was branded to their forehead. When this happens,
humankind tends to respond in one of two ways. People either
receive the branding and work hard to overcome it, or they change
the optics.

And what is the optic in this case?

Pregnancy at a time that society has deemed morally
inappropriate.

And where did they get this moral stance? That's just it—they
didn't make it up. It comes from God's Word, which makes it crys-
tal clear that sex outside of marriage is not what God wants for us
(Hebrews 13:4, 1 Corinthians 6:18, Genesis 2:24, 1 Corinthians
7:1-40). Today, this is seen as prehistoric and oppressive, but the
God who does not change (Hebrews 13:8, Malachi 3:6, James 1:17,
Isaiah 40:8) says it's for our own benefit. So . . .

We have a dilemma.

We either trust God on this one—or we change the optics.

And how do we change the optics? In my view, by softening
language and redirecting the focus. So abortion is changed to "pro-
choice," and our focus on the life of a baby is redirected to the
lifestyle of the mother.

I recognize that this is a difficult and contentious issue . . . and
a painful, personal one, too. Over the years, I've counseled hurting
parents, single moms, and those hoping to start a family who have
struggled with very real heartache from this, and I could hear the
pain of their voices faltering and see the tears streaming down their

faces as they wondered aloud how a logical, thoughtful, and even timely "procedure" could still cause such powerful emotion.

I wondered too.

From this, I learned terms I wasn't familiar with, like dilation and evacuation procedure and partial birth abortion, and about surgical methods (such as suction aspiration, dilation and curettage, and saline injection), pharmaceutical methods (such as Mifepristone and Misoprostol), and more. It all sounded so clinical to me . . . so detached.

But as I tried to comprehend these, I also started seeing that there was something more beyond the rhetoric, fighting, and political posturing around these, and yes, something more beyond the optics.

As a pastor and a dad, I will never forget reading about some of the "procedures" in greater detail, and by far, the one that broke my heart the most was what's referred to as a dismemberment abortion. According to LifeNews.com, this is where a baby's head is crushed and extracted in pieces.[16] I know this is hard to take, and even a simple Google search pulls up a lot of information about this with opinions on all sides, but to me, this wasn't just a medical procedure, and I felt it couldn't be explained away with clinical words and medical jargon. Remember "Sticks and stones . . . but words will never hurt me?" To me, this is where the sticks and stones come in, because at the end of the day, it describes metal forceps being inserted into a woman's womb and crushing the big head of a little body.

Abortion seems to divide our nation right down the middle. I feel strongly that we need to have much-needed conversations with one another beyond just the optics of it. But I also think these conversations need to be full of empathy, and as a Christian, I'm called to speak the truth in love and do it without judgment. I hope we—whether Christian or non-Christian—can find a way to talk about it, focusing on the *people* affected by it and not just an issue or an ideology.

More Than Meets the Eye

Ephesians 4:32 says, "Instead, be kind to each other, tender-hearted, forgiving one another, just as God through Christ has forgiven you." It's not just kindness for the sake of kindness. And it's not advocating selective tolerance. It's God's word telling us to be kind in the ultimate way leading to the ultimate kindness—the kind that forgives. The *kind* that overlooks mistakes and misspeaks, because we are all fallen creatures. And the *kind* that speaks truth and calls out the things in others that keep them from a change of heart and coming to Jesus.

As usual with God's word, there's a lot more in there than meets the eye.

I've been thinking a lot about this lately as our culture, on the one hand, continues its hypocritical advance toward favoring optics over substance and, on the other hand, calls out trivia while ignoring terror.

And in my lifetime, I'd never seen this whole train wreck on greater duplicitous display than with the constant attacks on a former president of the United States for his tweets, muffed phrases, name calling, and yes, sometimes flat-out mean and inconsiderate words. While that part wasn't new or even shocking—the ignoring of any honest evaluation of the good he did was so thorough—it was fascinating in a morbid kind of way.

And it was such an appealing bandwagon that I often found myself climbing aboard. Until one day I pulled away from all the upfront spokespeople from either side and looked at the issues and platforms of each party. I then compared them to the Bible, and a real awakening took place for me. The more polished political party wasn't always lining up as much as the foot-in-mouth party was.

Now, before you worry that you got tricked into buying a political book, fear not. This certainly is not that. But it is a reality taken straight from the pages of a children's story about the emperor and his new clothes.

The plot: an emperor of a city is fond of clothes. Two imposter weavers enter his city and tell him they will create a suit for him that will be invisible to stupid people. The weavers only pretend to weave the suit and present the fake suit to everyone in the city. Everyone who looks upon the suit is troubled by what they cannot see and whether they are inadequate or not. Everyone lies and says they can see the suit. A child breaks everyone's delusion by shouting out, "The emperor is not wearing anything at all!"

Too many today are looking or listening to only headlines, edited videos, fake avatars, or carefully scripted talking points. From these they take their cues, live their lives, and accept whatever narratives are offered from top to bottom. Rare is the innocence and boldness of the child in the old fable who is willing to step forward—away from the herd—and call things as they really are.

Just the same, I needed to stop obsessing exclusively about whether or not the former president's tweets were too insensitive or not PC approved and just pray for him as I had done for every other previous president in my lifetime (the Bible commands in 1 Timothy 2:1–4, "I urge, then, first of all, that petitions, prayers, intercession and thanksgiving be made for all people—for kings and all those in authority, that we may live peaceful and quiet lives in all godliness and holiness. This is good, and pleases God our Savior, who wants all people to be saved and to come to a knowledge of the truth"). And I also listened carefully for the truth. The real, unfiltered truth. The kind that sometimes hurts—but only in the sense that it indicates what needs to be addressed. It had been getting lost for me in all the prepackaged PC rhetoric. Time to get back to the truth our parents taught us when we were small children, and "sticks and stones may break my bones, but words will never hurt me" . . . unless we allow them to. Or, unless we use them as an excuse to do real harm to someone or something.

Also, by laser-focusing *only* on what the former president said or how he said it, we ran the risk of carefully concentrating on the game of hopscotch we'd set up on a busy freeway right before rush hour rather than the approaching vehicles sure to kill us. This kind of naive trivial focus might very well have taken our attention off of what things radical militant groups were *actually doing* behind the facade of a polished, eloquent, and extremely effective presentation. On the surface, the optics may have looked appealing, and the words may have sounded great, but what was really at the heart of it?

To be fair, we see this optical game being played on both sides— the same optics can be used for different narratives. For example, in the news, we've seen the imagery of tens of thousands of people marching peacefully as their hearts break and they long to see justice for all—not just some—people. But we've also seen, at other times, images of burning and looting, shouting and fighting, minus all that peaceful stuff. Over on the other side of the fence, we've seen patriots and people genuinely proud of our nation, marching peacefully, while a fringe group of them break away and overwhelm the Capitol. Which is it? Are they patriots or pariahs?

If we're repeatedly presented with only one of these narratives and not the other, that affects the optics. The negative imagery presents a completely different narrative and, a person could argue, one that is intentionally made to scare or omit any of the good in a situation. On the flip side of this is a narrative that is focused only on good, never showing a dark side or devastating events that could be happening in real life. It's an OPTICal illusion on purpose.

Either way—if you only get one or the other—this only breeds more division between people. Depending on what they see, which narrative they're following, nothing is solved, and nothing is changing because they're just following the optics without getting to what's beneath.

This is why so many people can align themselves with the surface optics of movements, positions, or protests without necessarily knowing what these are all about. A movement might, for example, have a moniker that presents great optics for mass consumption and acceptance, but if people were to dig in past the optics, they might learn that the movement's manifesto has less to do with the more widely known cause people have in mind when they hear its name. I think that some monikers are so well crafted that even raising questions about them is mostly off limits or, even more, can be considered as hate speech in some circles.

Have you seen me heading there?

Brace yourself. Incredibly polarizing movement name coming in . . .

3 . . .

2 . . .

1 . . .

Make America Great Again

Or MAGA for short.

This acronym stirs up so much emotion for some that people have been beaten for wearing a hat containing it.

Here's another one:

3 . . .

2 . . .

1 . . .

Black Lives Matter

Or BLM for short.

Did just reading that stir any kind of emotion? I believe it's meant to for both good and bad reasons because nearly everyone on the planet—other than psychos like white supremacists, skinheads, and neo-Nazis—would (and should) wholeheartedly agree with the statement that Black Lives Matter. Black lives matter. And what I want to share about the optics around this movement doesn't take away from that.

But you know that in this book, I've been trying to shed light on the importance of getting past optics (how things *look*) so you can see, recognize, and dialogue about substance (how things *are*). I want you to know that I applaud the support of BLM as a statement of truth and value it as a mission to bring attention and focus to the hurting and marginalized. After all, the heart of the Christian message is that we are all one in Christ Jesus. The apostle Paul wrote to the Christians in Galatia, "There is neither Jew nor Gentile, neither slave nor free, nor is there male and female, for you are all one in Christ Jesus" (Galatians 3:28). This makes it clear that *everyone* is included in God's kingdom. To this, I want to also add that for everyone to be *included*, absolutely no one should be *excluded*.

According to Politifact, through the Poynter Institute, "The Black Lives Matter Global Network is incorporated in Delaware, but it's a charity that's fiscally sponsored by another nonprofit called Thousand Currents. The Black Lives Matter Global Network has chapters around the country."[17] Some people have never heard this before. And I think a lot of people don't necessarily know everything about the BLM Global Network in general. We see the great optics in the name but may not be aware that it's also an official IRS-filed corporation with an agenda.

In reading more about it, I learned that it's a movement with clearly outlined goals that aren't only about the plight of Blacks in America. According to a piece by Soeren Kern, a senior fellow of the New York–based Gatestone Institute, BLM also seeks to advance other movements, listed, at one time, as follows: "Black Lives Matter seeks to replace the foundational cornerstones of American society: 1) abolish the Judeo-Christian concept of the traditional nuclear family, the basic social unit in America; 2) abolish the police and dismantle the prison system; 3) mainstream transgenderism and delegitimize so-called heteronormativity (the belief that heterosexuality is the norm); and 4) abolish capitalism (a free economy) and replace it with communism (a government-controlled economy)."[18] In Kern's piece and an article by Rev. Ben Johnson put out by the Acton Institute, I see language from BLM that is against the traditional nuclear family, and this, among other things, causes me concern as a pastor, husband, and dad.[19]

There's more, and I found that you really have to dig for the details, which requires some extra effort and is something people may not necessarily even think they would need to do. To me, it makes sense that BLM says it all; the name has good mass appeal and definitely presents the best optics. But, as it currently stands, not all Black lives are represented. Mostly absent is a meaningful focus or concern where some, like Walt

Blackman, African-American member of the Arizona House of Representatives, believe the greatest genocide of Blacks is taking place: first with the abortion of more than 19 million Black babies since the 1973 decision of Roe vs. Wade[20] (to me, that classifies it squarely in the camp of genocide) and next, with the heartbreaking crisis at near genocidal levels—the murder rate of Blacks by other Blacks in many of America's inner cities. It's almost always glossed over. Why does it have to be one or the other? The hurt and injustice is widespread. Yes, the hurt and pain in videos and on front-page situations is very real and needs to be addressed, but I think that when a patient is hemorrhaging, we need to address the location of the most massive bleeding first; otherwise, we're likely to lose the patient.

I have an obvious but honest question.

How do we fix a problem we're not supposed to talk about? Continue with self-serving optics? As you've just read, it's not working. Let me suggest an alternative—that we start telling the truth in love, no matter how uncomfortable.

Truthful, factual optics unfortunately do not often seem to be set forth by politicians or the media on either side. Instead, carefully orchestrated, edited, and selective ones are. They do this to bring about a predetermined and preferred outcome, understanding that feelings move the masses far better than facts.

It's nothing new. It's called "the straw man fallacy," which is the oversimplifying or misrepresentation of your opponent's argument to make it easier to attack or refute.

Still bewildered? I don't blame you—it doesn't make a lot of sense if you just look at the success rate of making decisions based on facts rather than simply feelings. Fact-based decisions bring about real change. Feelings-filtered decision-making only raises the needle on one metric—emotion. Therefore, anger often leads to outrage. Sadness leads to safe spaces. Criticism leads to cancel culture (I talk about cancel culture in more detail later). And so on. Nevertheless, the herd marches ever forward with rarely a single person ever breaking ranks.

Again, why?

Because if we can change our optics, we feel as if we can change the truth about our lives without *actually* having to change any convictions, or even the way we behave.

That's why virtue signaling is so popular today—almost no effort is required, and like the blood on the doorposts of the home of every faithful Jew under bondage in Egypt thousands of years ago, we keep all the scary stuff at bay because of the insider's signal on the doorway. Only, in modern cases, it doesn't signal alignment with God and his people—it signals appeasement to the culture police and keeps the Social Justice Warriors at bay for another day.

Let's be honest. Most of us would rather believe easier, tolerant, kumbaya stuff about the world over the tough issues that force us to confront what the Bible calls our "sinful nature." So we tend to filter out the bad and accumulate only what makes us feel better about ourselves—true or not. And, as if this weren't shallow enough, others don't bother with the truth at all because it just takes *too much effort* to hunt down the facts. Better to let someone else take care of that, and hopefully—if it turns out we got it wrong in this life—we can just blame the truthbenders when we stand before God at the pearly gates one day.

Good luck with that.

And all of this is because there is an uncomfortable journey into truth and some hard homework that needs to be done if you are at all interested in basing your life and commitments on facts and truth and on reality over optics. Like Neo in *The Matrix* saga, we'll need to listen to Morpheus—even though he could be a real pill at times (pun intended).

In the movie, the red pill represents an uncertain future—it would free Neo from the enslaving control of the machine-generated dream world and allow him to escape into the real world, but living the "truth of reality" is harsher and more difficult. On the other hand, the blue pill represents a beautiful prison—it would lead him back to ignorance, living in confined comfort without want or fear within the simulated reality of the Matrix. As described by Morpheus: "You take the blue pill . . . the story ends. You wake up in your bed and believe whatever you want to believe. You take the red pill . . . you stay in Wonderland, and I show you how deep the rabbit hole goes." Neo chooses the red pill and joins the rebellion.

We need more people to join the rebellion—not the anarchy but the rebellion. And to do so we'll have to start becoming more interested in facts than feelings. Sadly, most aren't. Feelings trump facts for many today. And relationships trump anything that's left. That's why identity politics (politics in which groups of people having a particular racial, religious, ethnic, social, or cultural identity tend to promote their own specific interests or concerns without regard to the interests or concerns of any larger political group) is becoming a more powerful influence than personal responsibility for current generations.

Many millennials love social justice and the social justice groups and friendships that come along with it. They even have an acronym for the recently formed crusaders for the cause—they're called Social Justice Warriors (SJWs). The Bible is big on justice. Not just social justice—*all* justice. Consider what the Bible has to say on the topic:

- How the just should live (Romans 1:17, "For in it the

righteousness of God is revealed from faith to faith; as it is written, 'The just shall live by faith.'")

- How God feels about justice (Luke 18:7–8, The Message, "What makes you think God won't step in and work justice for his chosen people, who continue to cry out for help? Won't he stick up for them? I assure you, he will.")

- Justice being part of God's character (Psalm 15:17, "The Lord is just in all his ways, and kind in all his doings.")

What does truth have to do with all this? Well, the problem is that without truth there can be no justice.

Why not?

Because justice meted out according to a lie or false narrative isn't justice at all—in fact, it's injustice. If you administer the death penalty against someone who didn't actually commit the murder, you've just handed down an incredibly prejudiced sentence. Again, unjust rather than just.

And if we go about social justice based solely on optics with a disregard for facts, we'll end up as USWs (Unjust Social Warriors), and that's the last thing really concerned, big-hearted, love-thy-neighbor people want.

My advice?

Take the red pill and read on. Answers lie ahead, but they will not always be what you expected. Press on anyway.

Not What You'd Expect

Many of the greatest heroes in the Bible weren't the most polished speakers—some were flat-out awkward—like the crybaby Jeremiah, the stuttering Moses, the sandwich-board bullhorn guy known as John the Baptist, or foot-in-the-mouth Peter.

And did you know that David was one of the original trash-talkers?

Yep, he didn't deliver his pronouncements through the Ivy League mumbo-jumbo filter. Here are just a few examples of David unloading on his enemies:

- "May his children be fatherless and his wife a widow!" Psalm 109:9

- "May his children be wandering beggars; may they be driven from their ruined homes." Psalm 109:10

- "I'll strike you down and cut off your head." 1 Samuel 17 (He said this to the giant, Goliath, in response to Goliath's own trash-talking.)

- Psalm 69 has a few as well. Verse 25: "Burn down their houses, Leave them desolate with nobody at home. They gossiped about the one you disciplined, Made up stories about anyone wounded by God. Pile on the guilt, Don't let them off the hook" (The Message).

- David was as real and transparent about his own sins as he was about the motives of the social media elite in his day.

And you might be most surprised to know that even the Son of God didn't hold back.

- Matthew 23:1–4, "Then Jesus said to the crowds and to his disciples, 'The teachers of religious law and the Pharisees are the official interpreters of the law of Moses. So practice and obey whatever they tell you, but don't follow their example. For they don't practice what they teach. They crush people with unbearable religious demands and never lift a finger to ease the burden.'"

- Matthew 23:16–17, "Blind guides! What sorrow awaits you! For you say that it means nothing to swear 'by God's Temple,' but that it is binding to swear 'by the gold in the Temple.' Blind fools! Which is more important—the gold or the Temple that makes the gold sacred?"

- Matthew 23:27, "Woe to you, scribes and Pharisees, hypocrites! For you are like whitewashed tombs which indeed appear beautiful outwardly, but inside are full of dead men's bones and all uncleanness."

But don't confuse trash-talking with truth-talking. Some of the very flawed and very human trash-talkers in the Bible were occasionally guilty of allowing their anger to get the best of them—Jesus, however, never freestyled. He said the truth because suppressing it was creating a false narrative that would cause even greater division. And God knows a divided house isn't stable. Jesus said in Matthew 12:25, "Every kingdom divided against itself is brought to desolation; and every city or house divided against itself shall not stand." Not "some will fall." Not "most will fall" . . . but *all* will fall

Friends, we are nothing if not divided. In fact, we are about as perfectly divided as possible statistically. Think about it: over the last several presidential elections, votes have split nearly 50-50 every time. We are not only divided. We are evenly divided. If we were to have a tug-of-war right now, rather than one side winning, there would be little to no movement. The rope would just tear (divide) and both sides would . . . what?

Fall.

What Jesus was referring to wasn't differing policies or views on how to manage the economy and so forth. He wasn't talking about mathematical division, either. He was talking about the kind of division between right and wrong, between following God and thinking *you* are God.

Part of what Jesus said is that a house divided is brought to desolation first and *then* it will not stand.

This is important because our selfie-obsessed, narcissistic, and anti-God culture is already in desolation. Many of the ethical, Christian-founded, moral, and strong institutions have already been laid to waste (made desolate). All that remains now is the fall. In fact, some of them have already fallen because the watchers on the wall were complacent. They were WINOs: watchers in name only. The "INO" suffix has been given to a lot of groups who at one point or another moved from the conviction of anything to the optics of everything.

Isaiah 56:10–12 (The Message) talks about useless watchers, "For Israel's watchmen are blind, the whole lot of them. They have no idea what's going on. They're dogs without sense enough to bark, lazy dogs, dreaming in the sun—But hungry dogs, they do know how to eat, voracious dogs, with never enough. And these are Israel's shepherds! They know nothing, understand nothing. They all look after themselves, grabbing whatever's not nailed down. 'Come,' they say, 'let's have a party. Let's go out and get drunk!' And tomorrow, more of the same: 'Let's live it up!'"

We're in a battle, friends. The very Christian values and principles that this country was founded on have either already been laid waste to or, at the very least, are beginning to crumble. Now is the time to push back against the tide rather than abandoning our convictions and continuing to reestablish ourselves further inland.

We need to get ready for battle.

Jesus wants a Christian delta force for this conflict—he's always been into raising up small, courageous, highly trained, and dedicated groups for world-changing missions. And he's always been up front about it. He's taken the Shackleton approach more than the "buy now, no money down, no payments for six months, lifetime money-back guarantee" approach to faith in Christ that so many churches and pastors adhere to today. Here's the newspaper recruitment add so often attributed to Shackleton for his ill-fated South Pole exploration excursion:

"Men wanted for hazardous journey. Low wages, bitter cold, long hours of complete darkness. Safe return doubtful. Honor and recognition in event of success."

Desperately aware of the dangers and odds that such an endeavor would entail, Shackleton could not afford to have even a single crew member who could not carry his own weight and even the weight of his brother, if push came to shove. He couldn't take a chance on posers and people pleasers. No optics-only for this expedition. So he put out a sobering, blunt, somewhat scary, borderline-ridiculous recruitment ad thinking very few would apply. As it turned out, he received more applications than he knew what to do with!

How is this possible in light of the premise I have been setting forth that people are addicted to "likes" and creating an image with great optics but that requires no commitment?

Simple. I never said that people were in love with the *method*—quite a few probably hate it! What they are after, however, is "being liked," and they've bought the lie that becoming a cultural people pleaser is a promising road to that end.

Please note, when I refer to WINOs, I want to stress that they differ from weak-minded, wishy-washy people in that they do not swing from one extreme view to the other and then adopt those opinions and convictions (on the surface anyway, even if they don't adopt them in their heart). WINOs are moniker people—everything they do is *in name only*, for optics only. Watchers in name only are holding on to the banner of Christianity like most hold on to the "Get out of jail free" card in Monopoly, until they think they may have to present it—in this case, to Peter at the pearly gates in order to *get into* heaven and *avoid* hell.

The Bible talks about WINOs quite a bit in places like the New Testament book of Jude, calling them—

- Clouds without water
- Fruitless trees in late autumn
- Wild waves of the sea
- Wandering stars

Then, later in Jude 1, the description is more blunt:

- Grumblers
- Malcontents
- Followers of their own sinful desires
- Loud-mouthed boasters

- People who show favoritism to gain advantage

Let me expand on this even more . . .

- Addicted to likes
- Envious of those who get more likes than they do
- Never satisfied with the likes they have
- Unable to live "beyond the optics"

Seems as though these Christians were a lot of things except, well . . . saved. When it came to being *real* Christians, the WINOs were actually CINOs, too (Christian in name only).

Watch Out for Termites

One of the reasons we find ourselves beyond even a post-Christian culture to an anti-Christian culture is that too many Christians are reactionaries who get passionate about the major upheaval of the day but almost always miss the little termites eating away at the foundation of our culture over the months, years, and even decades. The truth is, Satan is always playing the long game. He's been around a very long time and understands better than any of us that to bring down a godly people is done little by little rather than all at once.

I don't play a lot of golf—mostly because I'm not invited to play a lot of golf. I imagine the reason is because I'm not very good at it. I'm a fairly good athlete, so there were certain elements of the game I picked up pretty quick in the few times I've played, such as chipping and putting. But other aspects of the game—specifically the long game—are fundamentals of golf I never took the time to learn. As a result, I usually just walk up to the tee, put my golf ball on it, and swing as hard as I can. After seeing the disastrous results of that, I switched to swinging no harder than a seven-year-old, but with far more accuracy.

Bottom line, the Neanderthal/power swing usually sent the ball anywhere but straight, while the seven-year-old approach sent the ball straight as an arrow but usually no farther than the ladies tee.

So I was invited from that point on for comic relief. However, as with most comedic routines, once you've heard all the jokes, it isn't funny anymore—so people quit going.

Now, if I ever want to be invited back, I have a choice to make. Learn the long game and get good at it—or accept that I will always be a lousy golfer.

I'm content to be a lousy golfer.

However, I'm not content to be a lousy Christian. And I will never sit idly by, scratching my head trying to figure out why so many who call themselves Christians have all but given up on making an impact for Jesus. The stakes are far too high to mail it in.

Remember the section on the seven disastrous Ds? At which one of the stages do we need to be on the lookout for Satan's schemes?

Here they are again:

1. Disengagement

2. Disobedience

3. Desertion

4. Distress

5. Discipline

6. Desperation

7. Deliverance

Which one do you think it is?

If you guessed stage 1, disengagement, you're right. Satan doesn't wait to see which way the wind blows before shifting to the long game. He already knows which way the wind is going to blow—it's been blowing the same way since the dawn of time! So, goal #1 for the evil one: disengagement. Don't just file this somewhere in your cerebral cortex—be acutely aware at all times of your level of engagement with the things of God so you don't get on the disassembly line and start coming apart at the spiritual seams.

Basketball is another sport I'm not that great at. It just dawned on me that I said I was a pretty good athlete, and now I've mentioned two sports that I'm not very good at—kind of hurts my credibility. But the basketball deal wasn't my fault. I'm just vertically challenged enough to have figured out early on I would never be in the NBA. However, there was a time when my older brother practiced basketball every day for an entire summer before casually asking me if I wanted to play one-on-one. I'm more athletic than he is and was used to winning nearly every time we played any kind of sport, including basketball. (I know, I know—earlier you read that my brother won at everything—but those were the "Big Head Little Body" days. Things changed dramatically once I grew out of the awkward stage.)

But on this day he beat me like a drum, and I was stunned. However, since that outcome repeating itself was about as likely as actually catching a ride on Halley's Comet, I told him we should play again tomorrow. For the next hour I practiced making baskets, shooting from the three-point line, doing layups, and just basic dribbling—dunking wasn't an option for either of us. Then, as agreed, the next day we met again on the field of battle.

Here's how it went . . .

Game one: I won 21–10

Game two: see game one results

Game three: see game two results

What happened?

Two things: First, on the day that I lost, I took note of the one or two things my brother seemed to do well. As a result, the next day I was ready for those things. Second, I learned to move quickly to my right and do layups from the right side of the rim with a speed and consistency that he had no answer for. That's it. Nothing more than that. But want to know the crazy thing about that? I didn't take time to bring my left-handed dribbling up to speed, or the approach to the basket from the left side. Had my brother picked up on this, he could have just positioned himself in front of me on the right side and concentrated on shutting down that approach. I often look back on that and wonder why he never noticed that I never went to my left side.

Time to Suit Up

The stakes aren't very high for a half day of golf or in a friendly game of basketball between two brothers. But the stakes are Rocky Mountain high when it comes to eternal life and telling others about Jesus. And here's where the whole scenario gets just heartbreaking. Satan hasn't really worked very hard on developing his long game. Why should he? When most Christians wake up each day, they don't even consult the coach about how to live effectively as a believer for that day. They don't remind themselves that we are in a spiritual war—that the stakes are high—and that our enemy (according to scripture) "prowls around like a roaring lion, looking for someone to devour" (1 Peter 5:8). In other words, Satan meanders around observing those who look like they will most easily succumb, who don't have the patience to defend against his slow, methodical grinding away at our values, ethics, and dedication to and love for Jesus.

From the beginning of time, Satan has had a total of three plays: the lust of the eyes, the lust of the flesh, and the pride of life.

In Genesis 3:6, we read that "Eve saw that the tree of the knowledge of good and evil was good for food [the lust of the flesh], pleasant to the eyes [the lust of the eyes], and would make one wise [the pride of life]."

In Matthew 4, we read that Satan tried to tempt Jesus to turn a stone into bread (lust of the flesh), to look at the kingdoms that could be his (lust of the eyes), and to validate his mission to the people by jumping from a pinnacle and allowing the people to see the promised rescue from the Father (pride of life).

To this day, *every* temptation, *every* attack from the enemy, and *every* secular humanistic seduction falls into one of these three classifications because Satan has no interest in expanding the playbook. Why should he? These three plays are run at the NFL level while most of us defend at a peewee football level. We need to up our game—and we can through the power of Jesus Christ! Therefore, to counter the lust of the flesh, do what commentator Jon Courson suggests for each category. Do what Paul did when he said, "I don't allow my body to have mastery over me" (1 Corinthians 9:27). To counter the lust of the eyes, do what David did when he said, "I will set no wicked thing before my eyes" (Psalm 101:3). To counter the pride of life, do what Jesus did when he humbled himself and made himself of no reputation (Philippians 2:7).

And what about those who have no idea how the evil one operates at all? Well, they will simply be baffled as he drives to his right time and time again, scoring humiliating defeats over and over in the life of that naive believer. As I said earlier, Satan is playing the long game—but it's a very simplistic version of the game. He only drives to his right.

The Bible says in 1 John 4:4, "Greater is he that is in me, than he that is in the world." Christ followers have the Holy Spirit living inside them. That means that we should wake up every day, put on the armor of God (Ephesians 5), and expect to trounce Satan's plans at every turn—not just the right, but whether he goes right, left, or for three pointers; attempts to steal our joy; or even tries to dunk on us!

So, this being true, why are so many Christians not only woefully unprepared to play but not even fit to suit up?

Because they ignored things at stage 1 (**disengagement**); had too much fun in stage 2 (**disobedience**); blamed God for their melancholy and dissatisfaction in stage 3 (**desertion**); were too bound up in fear in stage 4 (**distress**); got mad at God for his stage 5 **discipline**; finally cried out in stage 6 **desperation**; and then got back on track once God **delivered** them in stage 7.

In real terms this may play out with a Christian starting to experience a lot of God's blessing and favor but beginning to take it for granted. They may still show up at church but only reluctantly, and they find it underwhelming and boring—they are beginning to disengage but don't see it for the danger it really is. Hebrews 10 warns Christians never to get sloppy about gathering weekly with other believers for church, because God understands how easily lone ranger Christians are picked off by the evil one—who is always more than happy to provide transportation when we are seeking to distance ourselves from God.

The coronavirus was one such vehicle to take us away from community. For a season that seemed to last forever, churches met online, and real community was hard to fully realize. We literally had to go after it with a hundred times the intentionality and commitment exhibited pre-Covid. And here's the sad truth—most Christians weren't that into it *pre-Covid*, so the likelihood of them powering up for community during Covid . . . not very. As I said, most weren't "up for it" pre-Covid. And while online church was novel and cool for a few weeks, the early online engagement most churches saw very quickly turned to step 1 (**disengagement**) of the seven-stage (Book of Judges) digression, with hardly a peep from most pastors.

God knew David was the type of person who would make a good king, because David already was a person who loved God with all his heart. This was David's first superpower. His heart was surrendered to God. Instead of his life being self-centered, his life was God-centric. And an individual centered around God does not worry so much about presenting the right optics—their concern is in embracing the right motives. The right heart. They're living to get better, to become more loving and more like Christ. In life's journey it's actually more common for them to lead with their struggles than lead with their avatar.

Not only this, but he also spent daily time with God. He sought the Lord with everything he had, all the time. And as long as he stayed close to God, he stayed out of trouble. And when he didn't, trouble was never far away.

Psalm 13:2, however, makes it clear that David was sometimes tortured by his thoughts (as most of us are, if we're being honest): "How long must I wrestle with my thoughts and day after day have sorrow in my heart? How long will my enemy triumph over me?" David said. The apostle Paul (who some refer to as the greatest Christian who ever lived) did the same. In fact, the entire chapter of Romans 7 is dedicated to what some have referred to as "vice signaling"—a sort of preemptive strike for those who want to shut down all dialogue of any kind with the deeply wise and incredibly powerful words of five-year-olds everywhere, "I know you are, but what am I?"

One of the reasons David is so universally admired is because he didn't focus so much on pleasing others and presenting the right optics. Instead, he ended up protecting himself from embarrassment by embarrassing himself first, or as author Greg Gutfeld says about vice signaling, protecting himself "from ruin by ruining himself first, publicly." Greg wasn't referring to David but rather *anyone* who wasn't petrified to share their struggles openly and honestly—or, in today's world, socially. David didn't seem to ever do this for some self-serving purpose or strategically; he was just a very authentic and real person.

Today all of this is magnified immensely on social media, where we see everything and want to be seen by everyone.

Your family could despise you—but if the cashier at Target recognizes you as the girl who did the incredibly dope "Wipe it Down" challenge—well, you could just die and go to heaven right then and there!

Giving in to the pull of narcissism and obsessing about ourselves never yields the results we are longing for. David figured out the secret of authentic living and finding purpose in an optics-driven world. That secret is . . . love.

A CHANGE OF HEART

Self-centered living results in inner destruction and broken relationships. Authenticity frees the soul and brings life.

THINK

- To become well-rounded, loving humans, we have to battle
  our natural, self-centered, narcissistic tendencies.

- In ancient times, Israel chose self-centered living instead of
  God-centered leadership. They used optics to choose their
  first king, Saul. His pride and confidence in his own abilities
  led to his downfall.

- Optics don't have to define who you are. Your potential isn't
  determined by how others see you.

- God looks beyond the optics. He chose David to be king
  based on the qualities of his heart. He is the founder of
  Opposite Day.

- God is the one who, regardless of anything we say or do, says,
  "I choose you." "I *like* you." "You are important to me."

PAUSE

- How do "selfitis" and narcissism figure into your own
  life? Have you seen them lead to any destruction in your
  relationships?

- In what ways do you have to battle self-centered living?

- In light of Opposite Day, how do you think God views you?

- How does it change your perception of yourself knowing that God sees the depths of your heart and chooses to love you wholly and completely?

CONNECT

But the Lord said to Samuel, "Don't judge by his appearance or height, for I have rejected him. The Lord doesn't see things the way you see them. People judge by outward appearance, but the Lord looks at the heart." (1 Samuel 16:7, NLT)

RESPOND

God, I am thankful that you look at the heart and not on the outside optics. Thank you for declaring Opposite Day over my life. You know that I struggle with self-centered living, but I want my life to reflect yours. I want to be a person who has a heart like yours, full of compassion, hope, and truth. Can you change my heart to look like yours? Can you help me focus on you and your truth, not just on myself? Thank you for always listening to me and responding with love. Amen.

Chapter 4

Likes vs. Love

The opposite of optics is authenticity. The bedrock of authenticity is love, because love is the bedrock of the human experience. And the source of love is . . . ? You guessed it, God! God *is* love.

However, finding real love with another human has never been easy. Just ask *The Bachelor*. No one likes to admit watching this "reality" program (least of all men), yet *The Bachelor* has been one of television's highest-rated shows for more than two dozen seasons. The idea is entirely implausible. For two months, people go on fake dates to places they could never have gone on their own, to do things they could never have done on their own. Nothing is "real." Even on "dates," they don't eat the date food—at least not on camera. Then, after two months of these "dates," the bachelor (or bachelorette, on the sister show) chooses a bride (or groom). To marry. For life.

In recent seasons, producers have put Christians with morals on the shows, and viewers responded, filling social media channels to

guess whether contestants would stay moral or not. It has become a
bit of a game to see who can get someone to give up their virginity.
Ratings soared when bachelor Colton Underwood literally jumped a
fence to get off the show after Cassie Randolph rejected him. He had
two other women to choose from but decided not to choose anyone.
Off he goes, over the fence, with producers and hosts chasing after
him in the dark, trying to save the show.[1]

In one of the highest-rated episodes, Colton came back and
convinced Cassie to stay with him. In the end, Colton and Cassie
got together, and viewers were left believing they lived happily ever
after. He got his pick. She got hers. It had been very uncertain for
a while, and that made *great* television—even if it didn't last.[2] And
they almost never do. *The Bachelor* tells today's story. Finding true
love is more confusing than ever.

I Heart You . . . Kind Of

With over 1,500 dating apps, the opportunity to find your soul
mate and love of your life can be completely overwhelming. Instead
of meeting someone at school or at work, or in your favorite bar, you
now scroll through countless bios on your phone. Instead of getting
your cousin to set you up on a date, you simply click the button
"hot" or "not" and take charge of your destiny. Or not.

First question: *Which app should I choose?* All the different types
of apps are mind-boggling. There are matchmaking apps. There are
hookup apps.[3] (Swipe right? Swipe left? Or how about not swiping . . . Is that an option?) There are apps based on religious beliefs.
Apps based on age. Apps for flirting. Apps for flings. There is even
an app for women who love guys with beards.[4] I'm not even kidding.
(*Really? You know those can be shaved off in just a few minutes, right?*)

While you have a much larger pool of potential love interests to choose from, dating apps can lend themselves to some awkward fails. Like the one where the guy used the line "If you were a McDonald's sandwich, you would be a McGorgeous!" No match was made.[5] This is not a surprise. His pickup line is laugh-out-loud funny, but there is a whole lot about dating apps that isn't funny at all.

Second question: *What if I accidentally invite the unwanted?* Matt Lundquist, a couples' therapist, said that dating apps tend to invite bad behavior.[6] From conversations with his recovering clients, he has heard tales of rejection and ghosting. Not to mention the crude come-ons and the lack of basic human kindness. Let's be honest . . . some of these apps bring out stalkers and psychos. One girl admitted she had a guy show up to their date and say, "You don't look like what I thought you looked like." He turned and walked away. #rude

Third question: *What image am I projecting?* It's possible that woman really *didn't* look like her picture. I know a 35-year-old who put up a 15-year-old photo. *You're 20 again? Really?* And what about people who know how to use all the filters and photoshopping? They're putting out optics that are nowhere close to reality. (What I don't understand is, if you don't look like the image, and you know you don't look like it, what are your plans for when the real you has to show up on a date? The other person is wondering what happened to those perfect teeth, those huge muscles, or that perfect booty you presented in the pictures.

Fourth question: *Is it for me?* You can always just *not* go out. And if you consistently put out fake optics, then perhaps you're afraid for people to see the real you.

While the longing for real love is real and as critical as ever, dating apps just don't tend to reveal much of the person's heart. It is hard to recognize a true opportunity for connection with a filtered photo and a witty sound bite for a bio.

Fifth question: *While I'm putting my heart out there, how do I know that the person I'm matched with is really who they say they are?* How do you navigate love when authenticity is thrown out the window? And in this crazy world of optics, what is real love anyway? How do you recognize it?

Real Love

In the English language, the word *love* has many different nuances. As a result, we have to rely on context and inflection to perceive how the word is being used.

For instance, if your buddy sees your new ride and says, "Man, I love your truck," obviously you know two things right away—it's a Ford, and he's using the word in a rather shallow and somewhat meaningless way. He loves your truck, but he's not "in love" with your truck . . . (especially if it's a Chevy).

Modern culture constantly chases a pseudo kind of love and wonders why it's elusive. People go through relationships like Kleenex. I love you . . . oh, no, wait, now I love *you* instead. (A whole lot of swiping going on . . .) This must be exhausting.

> "Disposable love is not the kind anyone is looking for."

An actor was married for 12 days before divorcing. I didn't know being married for less than two weeks was an option. Some Hollywood stars have gone through with seven or eight marriages in their lifetimes. That is a whole lot of wedding cake . . . and a whole lot of lawyers' fees. It's expensive financially and emotionally.

Disposable love is not the kind anyone is looking for. People don't get married with divorce in mind. They are looking for a true connection.

The kind of love that we all want is that deep bond between two people. The kind of trust and affection that binds people together, no matter what the circumstances. Real love that is nurtured lasts. It grounds us and helps us grow. That's the kind of love that comes from only one source—God.

Four Loves

Love is a multilayered word. In English, we have only one word that describes a lot of ways to love. In Greek, there are four words that describe different types of love.[7] I happened to have studied Greek *a lot*, so I will break this down for you. Basically, each type of love the Greeks identified is one we *all* want to experience.

PHILEŌ

The first kind of love is *phileō*. Phileō is a companionable love. This is where Philadelphia, "The City of Brotherly Love," gets its name. This kind of love is an unbreakable bond that occurs between two friends.

When a woman named Gerdi McKenna was diagnosed with cancer, her cancer treatment caused her hair to fall out.[8] Eleven friends rallied around her. Not just with love and support. They shaved their heads in solidarity and invited her to meet them for lunch, where they whisked off their hats to show their love for her. Their video went viral. A dozen bald, beautiful ladies is a powerful picture of phileō love and friendship. We all want friends that would care that much for us, to encourage and lift us up.

STORGĒ

The second kind of love in the Greek is called *storgē*. Storgē is a type of love that has its basis in one's own nature. Storgē is a natural affection or natural obligation, a natural movement of the soul for husband, wife, or child.

Lamont Thomas is a single dad who has storgē.[9] As he raised his own children, he fostered dozens of children over a 20-year span. But what he did a few months ago made headlines. He adopted five siblings, ages five and under, who had been split up in different foster homes. He said he couldn't stand to see them separated, so, "I had to help them." That was his storgē talking. He now has 10 adopted children and two biological children. This is one brave man.

We long for strong family ties. When those ties are broken, it is extremely painful. When they are nurtured and built up, it helps us thrive. Familial love is powerful.

EROS

The third kind of love is *eros*, erotic love. It is an overmastering passion that seizes and absorbs the mind. It is an emotional involvement based on body chemistry.

Hollywood makes millions telling stories about eros. Directors and actors tug at our heartstrings so we feel as if we ourselves are having our hearts break. Oscar winner *La La Land* was a deep dive into eros. The music! The dancing! The romance! More women loved this than men, and here's why: hearts melted when Ryan Gosling serenaded Emma Stone with smooth jazz. It's that simple. But, spoiler alert: their characters don't get together at the end of the movie.[10] This is almost as bad as Romeo and Juliet's heartbreaking deaths.[11] Romeo thinks he's found Juliet dead and drinks the rest of the poison. Juliet awakens, because she was really just drugged, and finds Romeo dead. "Oh happy dagger!" she announces as she takes her life. Basically, this story has been told throughout time, by Shakespeare, by the *La La Land* writers, by the ancient Greeks, and in every civilization including our own. Why? *Because we all want that happy ending when it comes to love.* We are in love with the idea of love. In our heart of hearts, we are hoping to find the kind of heart-thumping love that knocks us off our feet. But that's not necessarily how it goes.

Without the movie magic, eros isn't all it's cracked up to be. Eros, misapplied outside of marriage, has a very short shelf life. Its expiration date is directly tethered to those butterflies in your belly. Once those wear off, it's like those expired things growing in the back of your refrigerator—it stinks. There has to be something deeper connecting you to the person you love. Otherwise, we are back to those disposable relationships, scrolling through endless apps, looking for someone to fill the hole in our heart.

AGAPE

This gaping hole in all our hearts leads us to the fourth and final type of love: *agape*. This is a supernatural, against-all-logic kind of love. Agape is a love not kindled by the merit or worth of its object. It originates in its own God-given nature. This is the all-encompassing, life-changing kind of love that God has for us. It is the perfect love that we all yearn for, because it's what we were made for.

Agape love is the love that solves the issues we're facing. A great pastor and leader named Francis Chan wrote *Crazy Love*, a book about God's almost unbelievable love for us. Chan wrote, "He persists in loving us with unending, outrageous love."[12] There's a catch. The only way we can get agape love is to open our hearts to God. The funny thing about agape love is that it is impossible to fake. You can't manufacture it. If you don't have it, you're out.

In other words, agape love can never be just for show. It often manifests itself even in the most unloving environments. When we open our hearts up to the one who loves us the most, he is able to fill us up with his unending, outrageous love.

> **"The only way we can get agape love is to open our hearts to God."**

Unlike the other types of love, agape love has nothing to do with how you feel. It has everything to do with who you are and who you are becoming. As you lean in to God's agape love, the "super you" begins to fall away, revealing the authentic, real you, inviting you to love in a way that was never possible before.

Love Is More Than Feelings

It's hard for us to understand, living in a culture that teaches us from the youngest ages that we are supposed to *feel* our way into love. Everything we look at tells us to wait for those butterflies. Wait for it. Wait for it. There it is. That's what you're supposed to feel like. But God's optics show us the truth about real love. It's Opposite Day when it comes to real love.

The substance of authentic love is deeper than mere feelings. You might smile and nod at your friend who advises, "You'll know when it's right." But you know instinctively it can't be true. You're really thinking, *I thought it was right last time, and all I got was a broken heart.* That's because your friend's words are all based on feelings. Feelings can deceive. Feelings lie to us. Going to a movie and "feeling" heartbroken doesn't mean you *were* heartbroken. It's just feelings. Our feelings can change from moment to moment. Drugs can alter our feelings. Thrills can alter our feelings. You can eat a bad pizza at night and have bad feelings the next day. Wrong choices can certainly mess with our feelings. But real love is more than just feelings.

God tells us who we are, rock-bottom truth, not feelings. Gut honest: we are deeply loved by him. Then he tells us how to love him and love others by taking *action*. We are supposed to act our way into a feeling. Isn't that weird?

The choice to love comes first . . . then the feelings will eventually follow. This is the exact opposite of what we are used to. That is why when we are commanded to love, it drives people crazy.

You may be thinking, *Wow! How can you tell me to love my neighbors? I don't even like them right now.* Or *How can you command me to love a spouse who belittles me, or so-called friends when they treat me badly? That doesn't make any sense. I don't feel like loving those people at all.*

It's a pattern, and it works for everyone.

1. God fills you with his agape love.

2. He changes how you love.

3. He tells you to love someone.

4. You can start acting loving by the power of God in you.

5. Love happens.

None of this is because of you but because of God's love *for* you—and *in* you. His love fills you and begins to work in and through you. And here's a bonus. When you act your way into a feeling, the feeling comes. Your action of being loving, even when you don't feel like it, changes how you feel. But that's crazy, right?

Yes, it's crazy. It's crazy love. What's really crazy is that our culture has fallen in love with the optics of love instead of learning to love the way God created us to love so that we could be our authentic, true selves.

We don't love just for Instagram or for Facebook likes. Real love is so much more than words or images.

The real agape love that God has for us not only unleashes our authentic, real selves but flips our world on its head and turns our lives inside out. It is truly crazy.

Crazy Love

There is a common misconception about people who love God. People think they are crazy . . . but not in a good way. Have you seen the headlines churches have made by paying off the medical expenses for all the veterans in their community? Or when they pay all the lunch money due for local schoolchildren? Or cover the expenses of employees who are displaced by some tragedy? It happens. A lot. And it's all driven by the God kind of love.

And yet the only thing many people remember is going to a big city and seeing a guy wearing a sandwich board, walking around and yelling into a bullhorn, "You're gonna die and fry, while we go to the sky in the sweet by and by!" Super loving? Nope . . . not at all. Zero people enjoy being yelled at. What people want is *love*. And that's something that God has *in abundance*. God says that the greatest command is to "love the Lord your God with your everything, with all you've got, and love your neighbor as yourself."[13] He even says this is the first and greatest commandment. Why? When you love God with everything you've got, and love others like you love yourself, you get to throw out the rules. Why? Because you realize you don't want to hurt the people you love. You go above and beyond the rules. Which is what Jesus was referring to when he said in Matthew 5:17 (NIV), "Do not think that I have come to abolish the Law or the Prophets; I have not come to abolish them but to fulfill them." I like the way the New Living Translation puts it: "Don't misunderstand why I have come. I did not come to abolish the law of Moses or the writings of the prophets. No, I came to accomplish their purpose." Following a rule book (the Law) can never produce this kind of love where you want the best for others, where you care for them, where you want to help them.

Take me and my wife, Michelle. I love her with everything I have in me. It would be really weird for me to say I'm going to follow 10 specific marriage commandments to show Michelle how much I love her. Rules like . . .

1. Don't yell at Michelle.

2. Don't hit Michelle.

3. Don't scream at Michelle.

4. Don't choke Michelle . . .

I don't need those rules. Why? Because my love for her is all-encompassing. I want the absolute best for her in every situation. I want her to thrive. I want her to know that she is completely adored by me. I want her to be grounded in the knowledge that there is nothing I wouldn't do for her. My love for Michelle and her love for me go way above and beyond any rules like the ones I just mentioned.

The same is true for you. If you love somebody, you don't carry a bullhorn. You just operate out of love. You risk everything for them. You leave your comfort zone to fly halfway around the world just to make sure they know how much they are loved.

Jim and Elisabeth Elliot, heroes from a bygone era, knew the depths of this kind of love.[14] They lived it firsthand.

Agape Love Unleashed

Jim and Elisabeth met in college. They were passionate about God and each other. But they put off marrying, not wanting their love for each other to get in the way of their love for God. They were convinced that the greatest goal for their lives would be to share some crazy God love with people who had never heard of God before. They put their feelings aside and acted on that sense of direction.

Jim and Elisabeth went to Ecuador separately to help the Quechua people in the Amazon jungle. Over time, they realized their love for each other was part of the plan God had all along. They married in Quito. Soon they moved to a remote area of Ecuador to try to contact a group, known then as the Huaorani.

The Huaorani were a tribe motivated by fear and distrust that killed any outsiders that came into their territory. The Elliots decided to target them. They knew love was the only thing that could move these people from an atmosphere of fear, dread, and hatred and the unnecessary sicknesses and short lifespan that came from their Stone Age lifestyle.

With three other friends, Jim reached out to the Huaorani village for months, routinely dropping gifts in the river from a small airplane. Their wives held down the fort back at their jungle base. When the four men finally made contact with the tribe, landing the plane on a deserted beach, the Huaorani lived up to their violent reputation. The four young men were murdered by the tribe on the sandy riverbank.[15]

With his death, Jim left behind Elisabeth and their baby girl, Valerie. Naturally, it would have seemed right for Elisabeth to pack up and head back to the States. Who would want to stay in the place where you lost the love of your life? Or be near the people who murdered your husband? Why bring a baby into such a dangerous place where there was so much sorrow?

Instead of becoming bitter and losing herself in grief, however, Elisabeth's crazy love for God and people kicked in. She acted out of agape love . . . not out of feelings. She spent the next two years in Ecuador getting closer to the tribe that killed her husband. The tribe learned about the men who sacrificed their lives to share God's love with them. Overwhelmed by Elisabeth's love, the Huaorani tribe invited her and Valerie to come live with them.

You're kidding, right? How does that even make sense? It doesn't. Not in the way we normally think. But God's love defies our logic. And when we're filled up with his agape love? Our lives get flipped inside out.

There's a popular saying that "people don't care how much you know until they know how much you care." Elisabeth raised Valerie together with the children of the men who killed Jim and his friends. Elisabeth introduced hygiene, nutrition, childcare, and many ideas that were foreign to the hostile tribe. Her love for that tribe transformed them. Eventually, the man who personally killed Jim apologized to Elisabeth.[16] They became friends. News of this impacted more people in Ecuador and also at home. Back

> **"God's love defies our logic."**

in the States, huge national magazine articles carried the story. The Elliots were featured on the evening news. Elisabeth had a radio program for many years in the States to teach people how to love with God's love. Her heart reached thousands of people for decades. Crazy love tends to leak. It's hard to keep it a secret. Everyone who sees it *knows*.

David's Secret

David had that same kind of crazy heart for God. His heart was fully surrendered to agape love. In fact, in all of history, he was the only man that was described as "a man after God's own heart."

As a songwriter and musician, David couldn't stop singing about God's never-ending, steadfast love. In one of his songs (now called the *Psalms*), he repeated that single phrase, "your steadfast love," over and over.[17] He couldn't stop. He was giving tribute to God, knowing that even the ugliness of our nature can't make him stop loving us. Because of God's agape love, he takes action over his feelings, and he chooses us. In spite of us. In spite of our optics. Out of love, *God chooses you.*

God didn't choose David as king because he saw that David was the tallest or the best-looking. Israel already saw that play out with Saul. But David was considered the least of the brothers. God chose David because he was looking for *heart*. A heart that is surrendered 100 percent to agape love. It's not a 50-50, I'll-love-you-on-weekends kind of heart. There is no equivalent on the planet. There's no app for that kind of love.

Agape Love and You

Just like with David, just like with Jim and Elisabeth, God doesn't care about your skills and your smarts. He doesn't care whether or not you have charisma. He is looking at your *heart.*

He could give a rip about your abilities. *God chooses you.* He loves you. Are you ready to love God and surrender your heart? It's about time to shed the superhero cape, forget the "optics," and get some of that agape mojo.

A CHANGE OF HEART

Real love that is nurtured lasts. It grounds us and helps us grow.

THINK

- Modern culture constantly chases a pseudo kind of love and wonders why it's elusive.

- In Greek, there are four different types of love: phileō (brotherly love), storgē (familial love), eros (erotic love), and agape (God's crazy love for us and our love for him).

- Our culture has fallen in love with the optics of love instead of learning to love the way that God created us to love.

- When you love God with everything you've got, and love others like you love yourself, you get to throw out the rules.

- David's heart and life were fully surrendered to God and his crazy love.

PAUSE

- How have you found the world's ideas of pseudo-love have affected you personally?

- Have you experienced the four kinds of Greek love in your own life? How and with whom?

- Do optics influence your relationships with your friends and family? If so, how?

- Is your heart surrendered to God's crazy love? If yes, how has this impacted how you live out your life?

CONNECT

Jesus replied, "'You must love the Lord your God with all your heart, all your soul, and all your mind.' This is the first and greatest commandment. A second is equally important: 'Love your neighbor as yourself.'" (Matthew 22:37–39, NLT)

RESPOND

God, I know that I can't comprehend how all-encompassing and crazy your love for me is, but I am thankful for it. Can you show me how to love you with all my heart, soul, and mind? Can you shape my heart to love others like you love them? I want my life to be impacted by your crazy, wonderful love. I surrender my heart to you in this moment. Amen.

Chapter 5

Almost a Superhero

The world loves a good superhero. Since the release of *Iron Man* in 2008, the Marvel Universe and its epic gang of superheroes has raked in billions of dollars worldwide.[1] These numbers don't even include the DC Universe. (You can only choose one.) The market is flooded with superhero movies, TV shows, and cartoons. You would think we might get tired of seeing Black Panther or Black Widow save the day. But we don't. Hollywood keeps churning out movies, and we keep paying.

I've heard children ask, "Are they real?" and "Do you think Spider-Man will come to my party, Mom?" and even "When I grow up, I am going to be Captain America."

Just recently, I joked with a little boy who walked into a spider's web that he just might get lucky if the spider bit him and it was radioactive. I turned to him, grinning, only to see an earnestly hopeful face staring right back at me. He took me seriously, telling me he would call me if he woke up the next morning with superhuman strength and the ability to cling to the ceiling.

The pull of superheroes is real. It is amazing how children love these characters. They admire them. They want to *be* them.

Miles Scott, a five-year-old leukemia survivor, had a wish come true a few years back. The Make-A-Wish Foundation transformed downtown San Francisco into Gotham City and welcomed him as Batkid.[2] Everyone from the local news to the police department got in on it.

A call went out on social media for volunteers to show up downtown and help cheer Batkid on. Make-A-Wish expected 200 volunteers . . . 25,000 answered the call.[3] With the help of actor Eric Johnson playing Batman, Batkid saved a damsel in distress, threw Riddler in jail, and trounced Penguin.

When he was presented the key to the city at City Hall by Mayor Ed Lee, the crowds went crazy.[4] President Obama called to congratulate him. The world was cheering him on. Batkid saved the day!

The Great Escape

We're not that different from Miles. We would like to be superheroes, or at least have their powers. For a day . . . or even an hour.

Who wouldn't love to leave their day job and fly into outer space? Who wouldn't want to have their nemesis shudder at the mention of their name?

Every year hundreds of thousands of fans dress up as their favorite characters at hundreds of superhero and fantasy conventions across the globe.[5] For a few days, they get hyped up about upcoming movies and shows.[6] They meet their favorite actors. They pretend they are the heroes they wish they could be. And they buy loads of merch. Because we all love merch. But fun costumes aside, where does this great appeal for playing "superhero" come from?

Superhero mythology is the great escape.

Comic book writer Mark Millar says, "Good economic times usually signal the death of superheroes, and bad economic times see a surge in their popularity."[7] The more difficult life is, the more we want to escape. A bad day for the world is a great day for Superman.

Let's face it. We may or may not be facing a life-threatening illness like Miles, but Americans are pretty stressed out. In good times and bad, we always rank as one of the world's most stressed nations.[8] We are stressed about politics. Money. Pandemics. Relationships. Our health. Not only are we stressed out, but we are angry and sad. No wonder we want to escape.

Life can be difficult. No one gets through without a struggle. Challenges at home and at work are hard to overcome. We want to break free from the stress of real life and imagine a different scenario.[9]

You may be thinking, *I couldn't care less about Comic-Con.* But superhero tales aren't the only method we use to escape. Social media is one of the main ways that we escape reality. The average American spends 4.5 hours on digital media per day.[10]

If you can't be a superhero, at least you can escape your problems by creating a "super" avatar. Your "super you" calls you to escape with as much force as that latest blockbuster in theaters.

Of course, confidence doesn't come from social media likes, and fulfillment doesn't come from being viewed a certain way by others. But the siren song of social media lures us into thinking that maintaining a superhero look is easier than developing "super" character.

If you're sad, why not post a carefully curated story to Instagram to get Instalikes? Or if you're anxious, just lose yourself on Facebook

for an hour. Or seven. If you are feeling overwhelmed by life, or overlooked by others, why not just watch YouTube videos on auto-play?
The endless stream of entertainment will keep your mind occupied
and free from stress. Until they stop. And you actually have to live
your real life and face your real problems.

While it is fun to escape, real peace doesn't come from escaping
our problems. Hope doesn't come from pretending you are someone
else, no matter how cool your cape is.

The Hero Lens

Looking through rose-colored glasses is a Pollyannaish way to look
at the world. *Everything is good. Everything will work out. There are
no insurmountable problems.* As we all know, that isn't real life. The
opposite take is viewing life with dark, morbid glasses and a critical
lens. *Everything is bad. Nothing will work out. There is no solution
to my problems.* Both lenses are bad optics. Neither one reveals the
truth of the situation.

Israel's first king—Saul—lived his entire life going from one
lens to the other. At first he actually believed all the accolades people
were heaping on him and made sure all the social media of the day
reinforced his superhero status with the people. However, after
young David killed the giant, Goliath, and
knocked King Saul off the cover of *GQ*
magazine, Saul removed his spectacular
spectacles and replaced them with the
gloomy glasses that he would then wear for
the rest of his life.

> "Authentic heroes
> see the problems
> and issues in front
> of them with a lens
> of hope and faith."

Here's the thing. Authentic heroes
don't look at life with rose-colored glasses

or a defeatist view. They see the problems and issues in front of them as being very real, but they have a lens of hope. They face trials head-on. They aren't looking for a way to escape. They look for a way into the battle of good versus evil. They aren't concerned with looking good. They are concerned with doing good.

Real heroes don't worry about the optics. Mostly. After all, the optics are usually bad for heroes, right? Doom? Gloom? The end of life as we know it?

The day that David faced Goliath, his optics were looking pretty grim. Lucky for him, he wasn't into optics.

An Unlikely Hero

As an adult, David would come as close as anyone ever has to being a superhero. Everyone loved him and sang his praises. But he didn't start out as your typical superhero. He wasn't the biggest or strongest guy.[11] He was, as you already read, the scrappy, almost forgotten eighth son in a family of burly brothers, the one who got stuck watching the sheep. David was described as having a ruddy complexion. In case you didn't know, being acne-free isn't the best superpower for saving the world.

David was a shepherd. Nobody looking at David hanging out with his sheep would have pegged him for great things. His own family saw him as an errand boy who did the kind of lowly jobs no one else wanted. Shepherds have an odor issue in the field, and it's worse when they get indoors. It's likely none of his brothers hung out with him.

About three years after Samuel anointed him as the future king, David was still a teenager, Saul was still king, and Israel was still at war with the Philistines. The two nations had engaged in ongoing battles for years. At one point, the Philistines and Israelites faced each other on opposing mountains with a valley between them. Every day, the Philistines sent a spokesman down into the valley to bellow out a huge threat that the whole Israelite army could hear. According to the optics, the Israelites were at a disadvantage. Who was this spokesman? The enormous Philistine warrior, their super-hero, named Goliath. (Yes, it's true. David is about to meet up with Goliath, and "David and Goliath" really happened.)

Goliath was almost 10 feet tall, between 9'6" and 9'9" to be exact. He was decked out, head to toe, in bronze armor that weighed about 126 pounds, with a huge sword slung on his back. He carried a massive spear that was roughly 12 ½ feet long with an 18-inch iron-tipped head that weighed about 15 pounds on its own. Sounds like his muscles had muscles. He had an armor-bearer who walked in front of him, protecting him with a shield. Poor guy, it makes my arms tired to think of how huge that shield was.

For 40 consecutive days, Goliath walked down from the Judean mountain ridge called Ephes-Dammim and shouted up from the Valley of Elah to the Israelites who camped on the facing ridge. Every day he got closer to the Israelites and trash-talked them. He would shout, "Why are all of you coming out to fight? I'm a Philistine champion. You're just all servants of Saul." He followed up his trash-talk with some taunting. "Just choose one man to come and fight me. If he kills me, we will be your slaves. If I kill him, you will be our slaves. I defy the armies of Israel!"[12]

Garth Brooks came to Denver one time and played one show after another. The promoters kept adding more concerts because people couldn't get enough of him. Garth had a captive audience. So, too, did Goliath. The Philistines were loving every minute of this and were on concert number 40 without tiring of the repeated show. They were probably cheering him on, bolstered at what they perceived as the weaker opponents in the scrawny men of Israel.

For Israel, it was different. Saul and his army heard Goliath's booming voice every day, and every day they totally freaked out all over again, as if it were the first time they'd seen this movie. The ancient writings say they were "terrified and deeply shaken." No one, not even the bravest warrior, wanted to face Goliath in combat. And just think about this: according to the biblical draft report I mentioned earlier (found in 1 Samuel 9:2, in case you want to fact-check me), Saul was at least a foot taller than any other man in Israel. The most logical person to fight Goliath was the only "giant" Israel had—Saul.[13] I can't imagine being in Saul's army as Goliath called out for Israel to send over their biggest guy. Suddenly you'd find a fleck of dust on your uniform or see an oddly shaped cloud in the sky. Anything but look at Saul. The optics were terrible.

Goliath kept up his freestyle trash-talking for 40 days straight. He was like an NBA player who never gets out of breath and never loses his creativity for 40 solid days. Day in and day out, the Israelites heard the mocking giant remind them that they were scared, hopeless, worthless. The worst part is that they believed it. They felt every bit as sad and ridiculous as the giant said they were.

The Thing about Giants

Giants have a way of either paralyzing us or making us run. That's the way giants work. The giants in our lives taunt us morning and night: worry, sadness, anger, negative self-talk. Have you ever noticed how powerful these feelings and voices are? And they don't just come around once. Drip. Drip. Drip.

They are relentless. They get louder as time goes on. They hammer away at our hearts. They wear us down, ruthlessly trying to intimidate us. Leaving us so scared that we don't even think about facing them. We just want to get as far away as we can. But the voices echo down the valleys of our lives, keeping us paralyzed by belief that what they say is true.

Our incapacitating anger, our great worries and fears, and the things we believe are too overwhelming to avoid keep us out of the fight.

The problem is, if we don't fight and we choose to tolerate a Goliath, he'll take over our territory. He'll move in and set up camp. He'll destroy our lives. When we buy in to the optics of fear, worry, and anger, they keep us trapped. We sit mystified, wondering how to get free.

David's brothers were camped on that mountain of fear. They were probably scared, angry, and sad. Goliath had them trapped, and they didn't know how to get free. But things were about to change. They had no idea their kid brother was about to be the one to face down their greatest fear and set them on the path to freedom.

The Kid with the Biscuits

David's three oldest brothers were a part of Saul's army. Because David was too young to fight, their dad, Jesse, used David to deliver supplies. David would take time off from shepherding and take food to the front lines.

One day Jesse told David to take a basket of roasted grain, along with 10 loaves of bread, to his brothers and 10 cuts of cheese to the captain. While his brothers were fighting to save Israel, David was the original Domino's Pizza delivery boy. The warriors showed up to the site of the battle with armor and weapons. David showed up with a basket of biscuits and cheddar.

Just about the time that David arrived, Goliath came out for his daily head games with the Israelites. At the sound of his terrifying voice, the Israelites dropped their weapons and scrambled to their tents, petrified.

As Goliath looked across the valley, a sea of people were cowering, and David, God's man, was standing. It's not unusual. The ancient nation of Israel produced a lot of heroes. Moses stood at the banks of the Red Sea as Pharaoh's army bore down on him.[14] Esther stood against her people's enemy, Haman.[15] Three teenagers, Shadrach, Meshach, and Abednego, stood when King Nebuchadnezzar said to bow to his statue.[16]

As Goliath looked at David, he must have been scratching his head, thinking, *Either that kid can't hear, or he is a little nutty.*

David could hear Goliath . . . and he was getting mad. *Who in the world is this overgrown pagan talking trash about God? And why isn't anyone doing anything about it?*

King Saul had told his army that whoever shut the giant up would be able to marry one of his daughters and get a huge tax break (because *taxes*). David could hardly believe what a great reward was offered. He double-checked with a group of men. "What reward is being offered to the guy who shuts up the giant?" Those guys said the same thing.

At this point, David's older brother weighed in.

"Why are you even here?" Eliab asked David. "And who have you left your few sheep with?" (Who is trash-talking now?) This was a classic big-brother deflection intended to make David feel as small as Eliab did. Eliab was probably more than a little embarrassed that David saw him freak out and run to his tent. And more than a little annoyed that his brother was asking about fighting the giant. As if his kid brother stood a chance. Eliab was thinking, *Just hand over the biscuits and leave, David.*

David shrugged off his brother's taunts and said, "What have I done now? I was only asking a question." But his mind was already made up. If the rest of the army wouldn't fight for God and God's people, David would do it himself.

Giant Fighting

Every human being on that battlefield was operating with outward optics, including David's own siblings. But David was tuned in to the opposite optics: God's heart.

David didn't suddenly find some hidden strength. He didn't have a secret stash of steroids pumping him up or a cooler full of Red Bull. He just recognized how big God *was* and *is.* David's second superpower was faith. He realized that God couldn't lose. David didn't have to run away, because he believed God was who God said he was. God had a plan that was better than any human plan.

It takes faith to ask God to join you in your battles. The early church leaders wrote that "without faith, it is impossible to please God." (Hebrews 11:6) So, if it takes faith to please God, it only stands to reason that the more faith we have, the more pleased God is. God must have been pretty happy with David. David's faith was about to take out a giant.

King Saul must have let out a huge sigh of relief when he heard that someone was willing to fight Goliath. That is, until he saw *who* wanted to fight him. *That little kid? You've got to be kidding.*

But, instead of Saul fighting Goliath, he accepted David's offer to fight and tried to get David to wear his armor. A seven-footer's armor on a young teenager. It must have been humongous. First they tried the whole thing, then selected pieces, and finally, maybe ended with an attempt to see if David could even lift Saul's sword. David wasn't having it. Secure in who he was, knowing his own skills and relying on the power of God, David took off the armor and said, "Nope. I need to do this my way. I need to do this the way that God created me."

> **"When God is on your side, it doesn't matter what the optics look like."**

It's funny. The people who weren't willing to fight Goliath kept trying to force their optics on the one guy who *was* willing to . . . and who lived from the heart. David had discovered a life-changing truth. *When God is on your side, it doesn't matter what the optics look like.*

And the Winner Is . . .

David took five small stones and a slingshot to face a giant wearing state-of-the-art armor. Worst optics ever. Except when you are wrapped up in a strong relationship with a God who loves you and takes out giants on your behalf.

Goliath saw David and let loose huge guffaws that echoed across the valley. Then he added a taunt, calling David names and cursing him by the names of Goliath's pagan gods. Goliath said, "Come over here and I will give your flesh to the birds and wild animals." After all his hype and threats, Goliath just couldn't believe the other army was stupid enough to send an unarmed kid to do an entire army's job.

David responded with the most mic-dropping trash-talk of all time. He said, "You come to me with sword, spear, and javelin, but I come to you in the name of the Lord of Heaven's Armies—the God of the armies of Israel, whom you have defied" (1 Samuel 17:45–46). Takeaway for the day? Don't tell God how big your giants are. Tell giants how big your God is.

David wasn't done with Goliath just yet. He kept on: "Today, my God will conquer you, and I will kill you and cut off your head. And then I will give the dead bodies of your men to the birds and wild animals, and the whole world will know that there is a God in Israel. And everyone assembled here will know that God rescues his people, but not with sword and spear. This is God's battle, and he will give you to us!"

The war of words was won. Next came the war of weapons.

David took the slingshot he used every day of his life to guard the sheep and, with one small stone, hit the giant in the only place his armor left exposed—the middle of his forehead. David silenced Goliath. No more taunts. No more mockery. No more giant. Then David ran forward, hoisted Goliath's humongous sword, and chopped off the giant's head. The message was clear: *don't mess with the future king or his God.*

At the loss of Goliath, the entire Philistine army decided they really didn't want to be slaves and took to the hills. The Israelite army had their faith restored, remembered who they were (God's people), and gave chase. The Philistine losses were huge.

And Israel would never be the same. They were no longer on the run, looking to escape. David was a hero. The nation's faith was restored. God had come through and set them free.

Eventually, Saul went crazy with jealousy over David. What drove him crazy were the optics. History records a popular song written about David's bravery that went, "Saul has killed his thousands, but David has killed his ten thousands."[17] Today, we might say David got more "likes" than Saul did. David had a more popular

Instagram than Saul did. Saul was the Paris Hilton who was "all that" until Kim Kardashian came along. This left nothing good for Saul. Because his life was focused on the optics, Saul couldn't handle the lack of "likes."

He's not unusual in that respect. Today psychologists have a full-blown diagnosis for people who can't handle a lack of likes. In fact, one study confirmed the same brain circuits that are activated by eating chocolate and winning money are also switched on when we see large numbers of likes. Feeding into that, the study also showed that seeing likes on a stranger's post made participants of the study engage more with it, in a "follow the crowd" kind of mentality. It becomes a vicious cycle.[18]

This isn't a 21st century thing. It's almost as old as time. And it is what King Saul feared more than anything else in life—that the "crowd" would shift from following him to following the giant killer. Little did he realize (and even less do we) that his gut instinct in dealing with it would also lead to his undoing.

Whether consciously or subconsciously, Saul decided to apply cancel culture to the young upstart before he received too much traction to stop.

What is cancel culture?

According to Dictionary.com's Pop Culture dictionary, cancel culture refers to the popular practice of withdrawing support for (canceling) public figures and companies after they have done or said something considered objectionable or offensive.[19] Cancel culture is generally discussed as being performed on social media in the form of group shaming.

In this environment, we are afraid to speak, to joke, to vent, to express an opinion in general, because who knows who or what might be lurking around the corner, with a smartphone and a vendetta? Or worse—a smartphone and an unfulfilled lust for their 15 minutes of fame. Author Greg Gutfeld says that we used to call them narcs, hall monitors, snitches, tattletales. Not anymore. Now they are analysts, SJWs, morality police, self-appointed journalists, whistleblowers careful to have lawyered up before raising the whistle to their mouth. They are purveyors of truth and power. But on mainstream media outlets, I'm finding that, increasingly, they're regarded as "trustworthy and reliable sources."

Saul implemented cancel culture commands regarding David that lasted over a decade! When it wasn't Saul himself issuing the decrees, it was his entire army using identity politics in unison where David was concerned. Can you imagine how discouraging it would be to know your every word and deed would be met with bitter boycotts?!

What would Jesus say about cancel culture?

When our society starts looking for reasons to demean, marginalize, nullify, and eliminate, we need to remind ourselves that Jesus already canceled the debt of sin on Calvary and that coming to him in faith is the polar opposite of cancel culture.

Why?

Stay with me—this is highly worth understanding . . .

You see, God's standard is perfection. Anything short of this falls below his standards.

The word *sin* in New Testament Greek is actually the word *harmatia,* and it literally means to "miss the mark (failing to hit standards)." And what is God's standard? Perfection. Using this standard, all of us have sinned. Which leaves us in a pretty precarious place. So we need something and someone who loves us enough to lift us out of this pit of despair—someone greater than the accuser (Satan) and cancel culture Ninja. Fortunately, there is such a someone, and his name is Jesus.

Jesus isn't just King of Kings and Lord of Lords—he's the leader of the second chance society, which can best be described as the opposite of cancel culture. Cancel culture seeks to skip right over the first and second strike right to the third strike so they can "out you." Jesus wants us to know we can have a fresh start and that we can't out-sin his grace.

By the way, rant coming in 3 . . . 2 . . . 1 . . . if fresh starts aren't possible or even desirable, then why do we even have a prison system? Especially for hardened felons? Just to hold people in a sewer/solitary confinement for life? It would be better to die! If I knew that were my fate, I might find a way to end it all, and I think many would consider it too. The most common headline about those put away for life in solitary 23-hours-a-day confinement is their likelihood to commit suicide; at least part of a successful prison system is reformation and reintroduction into society for a fresh start—not just a permanent cancelation.

Faith and the Optics

The interesting thing about life is that there will always be giants. Fear, worry, and sadness have a way of looming large in our lives. There will always be stress and struggle to contend with. Facing heartache and fear is part of life. It's called *being human.*

The coronavirus was a huge giant, a Goliath that seemed to threaten us with death every morning. The optics were bad, and people didn't know how to see through them. The entire planet moved from a health pandemic to a fear pandemic. No one stopped to think what they were doing and instead reacted to the giant's threats. The fear caused by the pandemic resulted in people hoarding toilet paper or drinking fish tank cleaning fluid.

What that pandemic did to us has *never* happened before. It became like a political poker game. You don't want us to gather in groups of 100? Then I'll say 50. You say 50? I'll say 10. You say social distance when you can? I say stay six feet apart at all times or wear a mask! You say six feet or wear a mask? I say six feet *AND* wear a mask! So much of the crisis was perception—optics—and whether you believed people should return to workplaces and churches or not, there were always opposite perspectives. Neither side really seemed to listen to the other, and we became more divided than ever. We could try to escape, hide, or ride it out, spending all day watching Netflix or playing video games. Or we could learn the lesson from David to live from the heart—to enter into a love relationship with God, accept his love into our lives, embrace it, and act on it.

At the Summit (the church where I pastor), we knew that balance was the key during this time. The Bible tells us in Romans 13 that we are to listen to the authorities and officials that God has put in place (or simply allowed to be in place). Hebrews 10:25 tells us we are to physically gather each week for corporate worship and never get in the habit of ignoring this. And Matthew 22 contains the great commandment, the second half of which says to "love our neighbor as ourself."

How in the world do we stay faithful to all three of these seemingly opposing mandates? First, by realizing that God's word does not contradict itself. These mandates are not created equal.

Obeying God trumps obeying man—so we are to obey authorities unless and until they tell us to do something God forbids or not to do something God commands. Hebrews 10:25 commands us to corporately worship, but Matthew 22 commands us to love our neighbor at least as much as we love ourselves. Is it loving to put your neighbor in harm's way?

The obvious answer is no. And that is why we and 99.9 percent of churches worldwide shifted to online services for a time. After all, the direst predictions when we first learned of COVID-19 were that it might kill millions of Americans.[20] However, as more and more was discovered about the virus, we learned that those predictions were largely unfounded. Even so, by May of 2020, authorities were beginning to approach a line of demanding that Christians might need to stop going to church—something that God commands them to do—even if church services were held with far more safety precautions than stores labeled as essential. (Some stores were essential, and some, in my opinion, weren't.) It felt as if houses of worship were being targeted during this time, and I couldn't help but to observe that the protection of people seemed to be moving into the murky and manipulative world of opportunistic optics.

What does this do to the scriptural trifecta of Matthew 22, Hebrews 10, and Romans 13? Simple—it causes us to lean more toward faithfulness and obedience to the Hebrews 10:25 mandate to meet but in a loving and safe Matthew 22 way.

What about the Romans 13 command to obey authorities? This is God's desire until (as I stated earlier) the commands of secular officials and government go against the mandates of God. In that case, my response is the same as the apostles Peter and John to the governing authorities who told them to stop preaching about Jesus. Acts 4:19–20 contains their response as follows: "But Peter and John answered them, 'Whether it is right in the sight of God to listen to you more than to God, you judge. For we cannot help but declare what we have seen and heard.'"

David had a similar response when he heard the blasphemies and mocking of the giant Goliath. Rather than deem the fight "nonessential" like every other member of the Israelite army, David trusted that God would be with him if he stepped out in obedience rather than cowering in fear. He put action to his faith.

When we do, we put feet to our faith, believing that God is who he says he is. Even when we are scared. Our faith unleashes God's favor in our lives as we live according to love. Do what God has asked us to do. And do it the way God made us to do it.

We don't have to live under other people's optics. They never fit right. Adjust our view to the hero's lens of hope. Real hope comes when we begin to see things honestly, the way that God sees them. Know that God will come through for us time and time again.

And when we discover the love of God, understanding who God really is, we will discover who we truly are. Our truest, most authentic self.

Like David, *you are God's choice.* As God's chosen one, his child, powerful and strong, you can let your heart lean in to his love. And then . . . hold on for the adventure of a lifetime.

A CHANGE OF HEART

Authentic heroes see the problems and issues in front of them with a lens of hope and faith.

THINK

- We would like to be superheroes and escape life's stress and difficulties.

- We can be lured into thinking that maintaining a "superhero" look is easier than developing "super" character.

- The giants we face in life have a way of either paralyzing us or making us run. They taunt us with worry, sadness, anger, and negative self-talk. The optics of fear keep us trapped.

- David believed God was who God said he was, so he wasn't afraid. He faced his giant, Goliath, with a lens of hope, trusting that God would come through for him.

- When God is on your side, it doesn't matter what the optics look like.

PAUSE

- What kinds of ways do you try to escape the realities of your problems and struggles?

- What kinds of giants have you trapped in sadness, worry, and negative self-talk?

- Remember that God loves you with crazy love. How does that shape how you view your problems?
- What does the word *faith* mean to you?

CONNECT

The Lord is for me, so I will have no fear. What can mere people do to me? (Psalm 118:6, NLT)

RESPOND

God, you know every single battle I am facing in my life right now. You know all of my stress and worry. I know you are bigger than any giant or problem that I could ever face. Please strengthen my faith in you. I want to lean in to your crazy love for me and let go of my fear. Amen.

Chapter 6

Real Love and Authentic Friendship

"**A** real friend walks in when the rest of the world walks out," the old journalist Walter Winchell used to say.[1] If you have ever experienced the world walking out on you, you don't forget the friends who walk in. Those friends are priceless. You don't ever want to lose them.

At our core, people are made for authentic, life-giving relationship. Every human on the planet wants a good friend—or seven. Our lives are enriched by the people who connect with us.

From childhood on, we are slightly obsessed with finding a real friend. We want to hang out with someone who gets us and loves us unconditionally. Those deep connections give life hope and meaning. Best friends forever.

Holy Friendship, Batman!

The latest superhero blockbusters reveal our love for friend flicks. We flock to them in droves. They all revolve around the themes of partnership and love. *The Avengers. Black Panther* (Wakanda Forever!). *The Justice League. The Guardians of the Galaxy.* Who doesn't love a group of friends getting together to take down the forces of evil and kick some alien butt? Cheers break out every time they save each other from the clutches of death.

Superhero duos are even better. Batman and Robin. Antman and the Wasp. Rocket and Groot. (I am Groot![2]) Teaming up with a partner who has your back and whose strengths match your weaknesses, all while wearing cool gear and using killer tech, is a dream come true. These connections are magnetic. In classic French literature, we read the Musketeers repeat, "All for one and one for all."[3] (Free test answers: there were four, not three, and no, they weren't real; it's pure fiction.) Flash forward and Captain America tells his boyhood pal, Bucky, "I'm with you till the end of the line."[4] That kind of love and loyalty draws us in. The unwavering loyalty hooks us.

Obviously, superhero friendships are fantasy. But the dynamic between two people who care for each other and are willing to fight for each other couldn't be more real. It gets us right in the gut. We all want that kind of friendship.

A good friend is with you through the good, the bad, and the ugly. And the uglier the situation is that you survive? The more powerful the bond of friendship is.

Dynamic Duo

Jia Haixia and Jia Wenqi could be the world's most unlikely almost-superheroes. Born in the Yeli village in the Hebei province of China, the two have been fast friends since childhood. They are extreme tree huggers. They hope to save the environment, bring back the birds that have started disappearing from their village, and leave a legacy for the next generation. In the last 13 years, they have planted over 10,000 trees together.[5] They have a mission to replant the banks and wasteland near their river.

There is one catch. Wenqi lost both of his arms at the age of three when he touched an electrical cable. And Haixia, as an adult, lost his vision. He is completely blind. The crazy thing is that their disabilities don't stop them. They solidify their relationship.

Every day, for over 13 years, Wenqi has carried Haixia on his back across the river. Arms wrapped around his friend's neck, Haixia carries their shovel and pick.[6] Since they don't have money for saplings to plant, they are creative. Wenqi hoists Haixia up on his shoulder so that he can climb 20 feet up a healthy tree to find just the right branches to replant by the river. Haixia's climb is guided only by the feel of the branches and the sound of his friend's voice. When Haixia returns to the ground, the team digs together. Wenqi holds the shovel between his neck and shoulder, and Haixia uses his hands. They gently place the little branches in the ground, patting them down and watering them.

These guys are beyond inspiring. They make me want to go plant some trees and hug my guy friends. #bromance

The crazy thing is that they don't see themselves as being super or extraordinary. They just see themselves as being best friends. They make up for each other's weaknesses. Haixia says, "I am his arms. He is my eyes. We are a team." Together, they are unstoppable.

Five Super Traits

When we're friending, unfriending, and then refriending again, we make developing unstoppable friendships difficult. Developing lasting friendships requires stamina, grace, forgiveness, and a whole lot of give and take.

"If you want a friend, be a friend" is an ancient proverb, a bumper sticker, a meme. And it's the truth. When Moses led Israel, he gave them 10 commands. Jesus simplified it to the first and greatest command: Love God with all you've got, and love others as yourself. Incidentally, this is also the greatest decision you can make to create a great life for yourself, because this kind of love anchors authentic relationships. If we want friends who love us and fight for us, we have to become that type of friend.

Psychology Today reports five traits of integrity that most cultures value in a true friend: trustworthiness, honesty, dependability, loyalty, and the ability to trust others.[7] Building out these core values may not come naturally, but they lay the foundation for that rocksolid authentic type of friendship that we all want to experience.

Haixia and Wenqi have these traits down. They depend on each other for everything. Their work together allows them to do far more than they could do alone. Using their differences, they fill in the gaps of their disabilities. They have a great camaraderie, sharing both the struggles and joys of their work. Digging holes in the hardpacked earth isn't for sissies. And seeing your hard work surround your village with a new forest is just plain awesome.

The power of a trusted friend has exponential results. Their friendship is impacting their village, the environment, and the world at large. (Tree huggers, take heart.)

A good friendship is life changing. Research has found that true friendship has a ton of benefits. It can extend your lifespan, keep you healthy, and help your mind stay sharp.[8] Friends help you navigate life's struggles and cope with rejection. And a true friend can help you fulfill your destiny. No one knew this better than David.

His best friend, Jonathan, saved his life and set him on the path to royalty.

David's New Reality

David became the golden boy of Israel. Saul enlisted David and sent him out to fight battles. David always won. Saul gave David a high rank in the army, and the officers were thrilled. When he demanded that David win a battle against the Philistines before he married his daughter, Michal, he made it happen. Easy peasy.

David's life was Pinterest-perfect. He was anointed. He had won the equivalent of the UFC Ultimate Fighting competition, jumped 20 weight classes, and killed the giant Goliath. He went from being Jesse's forgotten son to living in the palace with the king. Not bad for a smelly shepherd.

Everything that David touched turned to gold. He was hugely popular. His optics went sky high. He had at least 10 times more Instagram followers than King Saul. But David wasn't watching those benchmarks. He was a man with heart. He had a love relationship with God and a capacity for deep, authentic friendships. History tells us that Saul's son Jonathan became David's best friend. Jonathan "loved David as himself." He gave him the robe off his back, his tunic, even his sword and bow. Jonathan loved David so much he made a covenant with him.[9] A friendship alliance before God. Best friends forever.

But it didn't take long before everything turned against David. And as far as Saul becoming the president of David's fan club? Well, let's just say that Saul wasn't really feeling it. Jonathan loved David. Michal loved David. Saul's own army officers loved David. The real housewives of Israel loved David. David wasn't just becoming a pain;

he was becoming a threat. In fact, Saul was afraid of him.[10] He knew that God was at work in David's life but not in his own. Saul stopped viewing David as the hero who saved Israel and began to view him as someone who was into throne theft. Then not into throne theft. Then into it again . . . So Saul would swing as a pendulist. Back to cancel culture. And then back to loving and accepting David. Oops, then back to hating him. Then loving. Then hating.

Seeing a pattern?

I've coined a new phrase for these people who swing back and forth from one extreme to the next. I just test drove it on you in the above paragraph. I call them *pendulists*. Give it time. It will at least make the Urban Dictionary before you know it. These people don't really look into movements, convictions, or even right or wrong. They just put their finger in the wind and see if they can sense which way the cultural winds are blowing, so they can get ahead of the next pendulum swing—almost always getting it wrong. But for now, pendulists find themselves not only failing to realize that the pendulum has swung but also failing to see that the secular pendulum is almost never where they thought it was.

This was certainly true for King Saul. He seldom considered the stellar character and loyalty of David because he was too blinded by his own desire to be the people's favorite. If he ever just looked at the facts of David's life, he would have never allowed the pendulum to keep swinging wildly to such damaging extremes. But that's just it—pendulists are allergic to facts; what motivates them is emotion. And feelings are the fuel that keeps them in orbit—far above planet earth and reality.

Pendulists swing on the power of drama and stall when they hit a wall of facts. Facts are like garlic to a vampire when it comes to group-identity adherents whose group of choice is pendulists.

Passion pushes the pendulum from one side to the other over and over again, like two tennis players who are not playing to win but rather playing not to lose. Pendulists play "not to offend."

As I introduce this new and troublesome group, some of you may be thinking that it's no big deal. If that's you, I want you to consider something with me for a moment and hopefully get yourself woke in a hurry. Almost every facet of leadership, guidance, teaching, education, and so on in our society has been captured by pendulists, from universities to social media, mass media, corporate culture, the Pentagon, and—you better hold on to your britches for this last one—even many of our churches. In all those areas, pendulists seem to believe that the pendulum has swung away from God, away from freedom, away from free speech and toward secular humanism, socialism (if not outright communism), and the labeling of all speech on the opposite side of the pendulum as hate speech. And in order to keep the pendulum from moving back, pendulists have gone after all the "isms."

> **"Pendulists swing on the power of drama and stall when they hit a wall of facts."**

Pete Hegseth talks about this in his book *American Crusade* in a political reference to those who would undermine our country, but I think it goes further than that. When pendulists go after the "isms," they are going after our entire being—body, soul, and spirit.

Hegseth goes on to say that anti-Americans have taken over a lot of the "isms"—but again, it's more than "a lot," and it's about a whole lot more than America. I looked at a list of hundreds of "isms" and was shocked to discover that just about *every "ism" you can think of* has been on the pendulists' takeover agenda, including socialism, globalism, pantheism, fanaticism, liberalism, multiculturalism, fascism, communism, materialism, narcissism, alarmism, Maoism, atheism, environmentalism, secularism, Islamism, progressivism, cronyism, Fabianism, totalitarianism, elitism, defeatism, collectivism, despotism, establishmentarianism, feminism, fetishism, heathenism, homoeroticism, humanism, virilism, transvestism, transsexualism—about the only "ism" they seem uninterested in is ventriloquism. But I'm sure they'll add it soon enough. Putting words in other people's mouths is too much of a favorite to pass that one up.

Oops, I forgot truism—they hate that one as well.

If those opposed to authenticity and godliness have already captured all these "isms," what hope is there? If pendulists have really shored up all the loose "ism" ends we can think of, is there really much prospect at all of turning things around?

Yep.

Because one "ism" trumps them all.

Theism—the doctrine or belief in the existence of a God, the one true God, the God of the Bible (God the Father) and his one and only Son, Jesus Christ.

Besides, the "isms" are just the institutions that pendulists *have* captured; the most powerful one of all remains uncaptured. Jesus made it plain that the most powerful institution on earth is his Bride—the Church. As long as the Church stays strong and true to biblical principles, all these hijacked institutions combined will not be able to withstand her.

Jesus confirmed as much when he said, in Matthew 16:18, regarding the Church, that the very "gates of hell will not be able to prevail against her."

But in order to tear down the gates and defeat the enemy, we need to locate them first and find out where most of the workers are being concentrated in the construction, shoring up, and expansion of said gates. Expose these—find the optics around these—and the construction project will grind to a halt.

But it won't be easy. Unfortunately, when "pendulists" are called out, they become masters of deflection, choosing mostly to employ the childish tactic we all learned around the age of five that I talked about before—"I know you are, but what am I?!" We really need to come up with a one- or two-word moniker for this to bluntly communicate what's really going on . . . wait, we may already have it.

Projection—a defense mechanism in which the ego defends itself against unconscious impulses or qualities by denying their existence in themselves and attributing them to others.

But keep in mind that projection merely tosses the hot potato to someone else (who tosses it to someone else, who tosses it to someone else, and so on). It never seeks to cool things down. I think this is sad because as long as the issue is too hot to handle, it will be doomed to be eternally tossed.

I have a better idea. Why don't we seek God in the things that divide us? This includes the hot potato subjects like identity politics, social justice, political correctness, radical environmentalism, gender neutrality, cancel culture, virtue signaling, diversity worship, faith, authority aversion, and so on. I believe we need to find a way to see through the optics of these and get to what matters most.

Okay, that was free—back to Saul and David . . .

Ever since God's spirit left him, Saul had been a wreck. He was anxious and angry. He asked David to play his lyre for him, to help calm his nerves. David was a phenomenal musician. (Yes, besides all of the above, he was also a rock star.) David played his music and it helped Saul's head for a while . . . until it didn't.

Everything about David's life, his victories in battle, his ability to win the affections of Saul's own son, his popularity, and especially his lyre playing, worked on Saul's last nerve. He went from basically tweeting against David every chance he got to trying to murder David. One afternoon, when David was strumming some smooth jazz, Saul picked up his spear and hurled it at David, right in front of everyone.[11] David barely escaped. That must have been the most-watched episode of that season.

David's days of Instagram likes and viral tweets were coming to an end. After two more attempts on his life, David was on the run.

God "Likes" David

The optics for David turned grim. He no longer had the favor of the king, which is rough when you are living in the king's house, best friends with his son, and married to his daughter. David was officially Saul's enemy. The most powerful man in the land had it out for him. But David had something that Saul didn't—an alliance with God. David was a man "after God's own heart." God really "liked" David. And when God is on your side, Opposite Day is just around the corner.

God had plans and a purpose for David that Saul couldn't touch. His love anchored David. When God "likes" you, it's not like the tweets, fist bump emojis, virtual high fives, or "likes" that the world gives. David could trust God's "like." He didn't understand why Saul was trying to kill him, but he knew—absolutely *knew*—that God would protect him. And God did. He used David's best friend to do it. Jonathan was with him till the end of the line.

Authentic friendships that are based on real love, agape love, the love of God, go beyond shared interests and hangout nights. These friendships are far above temporary bromances and fangirling (yep, it's a thing). Going from "likes" into authentic relationship is like going from cheap dollar-store earbuds to a pair of Sony noise-canceling, highdef headphones. You turn up the volume and bliss out, thinking, *How did I live without these?* Authentic friendships are cemented by an unbreakable bond, powerful enough to withstand life's most desperate moments.

Cecil and Glenn became best friends in third grade. It's not hard to imagine the kind of friendship they had. Sharing the ball in sports. Sharing the controller in their first videogame. Sharing a bag of chips at lunch. The decades solidified their bond. But as Cecil aged, his health took a bad turn. One of his kidneys began to fail. Considered critical, he was eligible for an immediate kidney transplant, but the wait was three to five years. In desperation for her dad's life, Cecil's daughter offered her kidney, only to find she wasn't a match. That's when the eight-year-old inside of Glenn took matters into his own hands. This wasn't exactly sharing a sandwich on the playground, but Glenn found out he was a good match. He did it. He had two kidneys and gave Cecil one. His selfless decision saved Cecil's life.[12] It was a superhero move, but Glenn didn't see it that way. He simply saw it as an opportunity to help a friend. Trustworthy. Dependable. Honest. Loyal. Glenn's love for his friend changed Cecil's destiny and gave him a new chance at life.

Jesus is the one who said, "There is no greater love than to lay down one's life for one's friends." Glenn and Cecil get this. Crisis moments define our relationships. Will we come through for each other? In the darkest moments of life, are we there to offer each other hope? Do we throw out a lifeline? Bring a meal? Encourage each other? Give a kidney?

Jonathan and David had that kind of unbreakable alliance.

They were a superhero duo, unstoppable in their love for each other. Jonathan's dad declared war on David, but that didn't change Jonathan's heart. When the whole world walked out on David, Jonathan walked in.

Jonathan and David

After several murder attempts on David's life (because evidently kings are allowed to kill people for no reason), Saul was over it. He wanted David gone. He put out a hit on his son-in-law. Saul invited David to his feast at the New Moon banquet (think Thanksgiving). It felt like another setup, so David asked Jonathan to find out what his dad was up to. They made a plan to meet up in a field the following day. There was Jonathan, the heir to the throne, the young man who had been groomed from childhood to be king, and he's talking to his shepherd-boy-warrior-rock-star friend. Instead of being jealous of David, Jonathan basically said, "May God bless you as you become king, and when you do, please always show kindness to me and my family."

Then they parted. And Jonathan went into the palace ready to risk his life to save David's. And ready to give up his crown to ensure David got it. Jonathan put himself at great risk for his friend. He was risking his dad's approval and his own safety. But Jonathan had a different motivation than approval or ambition. Jonathan loved God. And Jonathan loved David as he loved himself. David was more than a friend, closer than a brother. And for David, the forgotten younger brother, Jonathan was the brother he'd never had in his own.

David thwarted Saul's plans to kill him by skipping the New Moon banquet. When he didn't show up, Saul was livid. The nerve of David—not being more helpful in the implementation of his own assassination. Saul told Jonathan that he'd never wear the crown as long as David was alive. David had to die. Jonathan asked, "Why should he be put to death? What has he done?" Saul was so angry he almost ended his son's chance for the crown right then. He chucked his spear at Jonathan.

Jonathan saw what was coming for David. He knew David had to run.

After dinner, Jonathan walked out to the field to find David in the hiding place they'd chosen. He told David that it was real; Saul was intent on murdering him. As a result, David would have to run. They'd most likely never see each other again. The two were heartbroken. They both wept. David cried the hardest. He was losing his best friend, closer than his own brothers, and leaving his wife and his life to go on the run. There was nothing that could heal a wound like that.

The Ties That Bind

The ties of friendship often lead to new family members. As writer Jess C. Scott says, "Friends are family that you choose."[13] Sometimes your friends choose you first.

When 40-year-old Elizabeth found out that she had terminal cancer, she had one request for Laura, her childhood best friend. Elizabeth asked Laura to raise her four daughters. It wasn't a small ask or a simple pinky promise. It was a life-altering decision, and Laura made the commitment in a moment. Because she loved Elizabeth. Those four little girls became her family.[14]

David's friendship with Jonathan was like that. A few years after they parted, Jonathan died in battle alongside his father. David became king. The memory of that friendship never left

David. About 15 years into his reign, David's thoughts turned again toward his friend Jonathan. He asked his officials, "Are there any survivors from Saul's family?"[15] His servants searched high and low and found Jonathan's grandson, Mephibosheth. Mephibo-what? Wow! Say that name three times fast! This guy has Rumpelstiltskin beat for weirdest name ever.

Anyway, Mephibosheth seemed to sense he was persona non grata and stayed as far away from David as he could get. Meph (yeah, I'm not going to keep typing that whole name) was living in a dry, rocky, sandy wilderness called Pasture-less. It had to be a really bad place if they didn't even *try* to name it "Whispering Pines" or "Rolling Hills." Why did Meph leave the comfort of the capital city for such a desolate place? Because he was scared to death of the new king. In that day, if a king from a different family came to power, he would eliminate anyone who could claim to be the rightful heir to the throne. He'd kill all the family members of the previous king. Meph naturally thought David was out to kill him.

That wasn't Meph's only problem. He had a rough life all around. In his language, Meph actually meant "shameful breath." How would you like to be named *Halitosis*? Hal for short. Or *Morning Breath*? Hi, Morrie. More than likely, Meph's name meant that he had asthma, or some other breathing ailment. So, he was chronically sick *and* had a terrible name.

On top of that, he was lame in both feet. When Saul and Jonathan died in battle, Meph was just five years old. Fearing what was coming, his nanny scooped him up to rush him to safety, but in her haste, she tripped and Meph fell. So now he had a spinal injury, too. And there sits Meph—the former heir to the throne; he can't breathe, can't walk, lives in a desert, and is scared to death. It had to feel worse than being "unliked" by a million people all at the same time. In fact, Meph felt so worthless, useless, hopeless, and canceled, that he gave himself a new name, calling himself a "dead dog."

David's officials told him they found a relative of Jonathan's, and David was jubilant. *Jonathan's grandson? You kidding me? Well, bring him. Get him here!*

David didn't see Meph the way Meph saw Meph. Meph had been canceled for years, but fortunately, true believers don't participate in cancel culture because the Lord didn't cancel them. They know God's forgiveness firsthand and, as a result, tend to be forgiving themselves. David saw his best friend Jonathan's grandkid and a chance to honor his oath to the best friend he ever had or would *ever* have. David pulled out all the stops. He showered Meph with kindness, Jonathan-style. David restored all of Saul's former lands to Meph. Seeing his disability and hay fever, David told Meph not to bother to go to the fields. David ordered his own servants to farm Meph's land. David ensured there was food for Meph's entire family, but he invited Meph personally to eat with him at his own royal table. David practically adopted Meph. Talk about Opposite Day.

David took care of Meph for Jonathan's sake. David showed Meph grace because Jonathan had shown David grace. David was merciful because of all the mercy that his best friend had poured out on him. David loved Jonathan to the end of the line, and that overflowed onto his grandson. David took care of Meph for the rest of his life.[16]

God "Likes" You

Just in case you were wondering what this has to do with you, there is someone who wants to take care of you for the rest of your days, too. God "likes" you the same way he "liked" David. He wants to call you "friend." Whatever is going on in your life now or in the past—if you were dropped on your head as a kid, have chronic problems, feel worthless—whatever the optics, God is on your side. When it feels like the whole world is walking out on you, God is walking in. He has a purpose for your life. He's made plans for you.

One of those plans is for you to cultivate authentic relationships, first with God, then with those around you. God knows how much you need the anchor of his love and the unstoppable kindness of people who love you unconditionally.

You were made for true connection, not just for "likes." When you "friend" God, connect with him, pursue him, you will find, like David and Jonathan did, that the depths of his love for you are endless and ageless.

The more you hang with God, the more you'll learn to love the way he loves. The more his love gets inside you, the more you'll act like him. Honest. Dependable. Loyal. Trustworthy. Able to trust God and others. God wants to pull out all the stops for you. He wants to shower you with kindness. He wants to move you beyond the pseudo-family and "friends" of an avatar world and make you truly family. You don't have to be a super anything. He already has a place at the table for you. And you will know, deep in your gut, that he is with you to the end of the line.

> "You were made for true connection, not just for 'likes.'"

And best of all? He is never going to turn you away just because you make some stupid, inane, asinine, half-witted, brainless, ill-advised, uneducated, mindless, senseless, loser mistake. I've done it. We all do it. You won't believe how bad David did it.

A CHANGE OF HEART

> **"A real friend walks in when the rest of the world walks out."**
>
> —WALTER WINCHELL

THINK

- At our core, people are made for authentic, life-giving relationship. Our lives are enriched by the people who connect with us.

- Developing lasting friendships requires stamina, grace, and forgiveness.

- The five traits of integrity that most cultures value in a true friend are trustworthiness, honesty, dependability, loyalty, and the ability to trust others.

- A true friend can help you fulfill your God-given destiny.

- God's plans and purpose for us are untouchable by anyone else.

- God wants to take care of you for the rest of your days.

PAUSE

- Are you the type of friend that walks in when others walk out? If so, how and when did you demonstrate this?

- Crisis moments define our relationships. How have others stepped in and shaped your life in moments of crisis?

- Have you ever written someone off because you got caught up in cancel culture? How would Jesus want you to handle it instead?

- Jonathan loved David more than he loved himself. How did Jonathan throw out all the rules with his love? How did this love ultimately affect Mephibosheth?

- The more you hang out with God, the more you love others as he does. In what ways has his love influenced you? How would you like it to affect you in the future?

CONNECT

There is no greater love than to lay down one's life for one's friends. (John 15:13, NLT)

RESPOND

God, I want your crazy love for me to impact how I love others. I want to be the kind of friend who walks in when others walk out. Develop my character in a way that is pleasing to you, and help me to love my friends the way that you love me. Shape me with your mercy and hope. Let it overflow in my relationships, impacting future generations. Amen.

Chapter 7

Love, Kryptonite, and Snowballs

C hris Stanley, a mineralogist from London's Natural History museum, was stumped. He had received a mineral sample from the Rio Tinto mining group that was collected in an unknown sample of rock from a mine in Serbia. Stanley had an extensive knowledge of minerals but had never come across one like this before. A dull white color, it was nothing special to look at. Under an ultraviolet light, it had a light pinkish-orange glow.[1]

Analyzing its composition, Stanley discovered it had a chemical formula of $LiNaSiB_3O_7(OH)$. Yeah, I know. Means nothing to me either, but here's what it is for all you science nerds . . . sodium lithium boron silicate hydroxide. Still nothing? So he did what all great scientists do. He googled it (because Google). The results could be called super. The Rio Tinto miners had discovered kryptonite.[2] Well, not really—but kind of. Lithium and boron, both relatively rare, are industrially important elements. Lithium is used for lithium batteries, and boron is used in alloys, ceramic, glasses, and other applications.

Stay Strong, Superman!

The kryptonite from Serbia was a slightly different chemical compound from the sample stolen by Lex Luthor in *Superman Returns*. It didn't contain fluorine. But it did spark the imaginations of wannabe superheroes around the world. The fantastic glowing green mineral that dropped Superman like a rock and robbed him of his powers has become a part of our cultural vernacular.

Any weakness that can drain you, or any superpower, of your willpower, logic, or decision-making abilities is your personal *kryptonite*. Your kryptonite might be NASCAR. Milk chocolate. Reality television. Your ex. It's different for each of us.

One thing we all have in common, though, is that we're not perfect. We all struggle. We all have weaknesses. We all have temptations and days where we eat our way through the fridge, then polish off a tub of ice cream.

Even those of us with the best intentions can be taken out at the knees by a weakness or three.

Viva Las Vegas

Here's a story that sounds like a bad *Saturday Night Live* sketch. In 2018, two nuns were arrested in Torrance, California, for embezzling funds from the Catholic school where they had taught for over 20 years.[3] Auditors found the fraud the year after the two friends retired. Over a 10-year period, it amounted to half a million dollars. Where did they spend it? Not clothes, right? No, they spent it on lavish trips . . . to Vegas . . . to gamble. Two high-roller nuns going nuts at the roulette wheel. What a visual.

After being discovered, it was rough for the nuns to answer to the police, to their holy order, and to others. The pair sent a letter admitting their guilt, apologizing to the students and their families, and asking for forgiveness. What happens in Vegas . . . never stays in Vegas. Vegas was kryptonite for the two nuns.

It's a sad story, and yet when the people we trust the most betray us, it's heartbreaking. The two women probably went through the painstaking process of becoming a nun because they loved God and wanted to honor him with their lives. They probably taught for two decades with the best of intentions. So, what was the moment that set them on the road to Sin City? The same moment we have all faced multiple times over. It is the moment when something catches our eye, or when we feel as if we're not getting what we want or deserve. It's the time we think life, God, our family, our job is somehow ripping us off. It's that flash when we decide to take matters into our own hands. It's not usually a giant plunge into bad decision-making but a tiny sidestep that leads to another tiny sidestep. And another. And another.

We all know the feeling of wanting more than we have. We know what it feels like to long for something that is out of reach. We have all made a bad choice and then followed it up with another bad choice. Suddenly, we find ourselves knee deep in disgrace, lost in our kryptonite, our own version of Vegas.

I know what it's like to live with regret and deep shame. I've made decisions I'm not proud of, things I can't go back and change. You're human, so you've also made decisions that have caused shame and regret. You are probably thinking about them right now.

Welcome to the world. This is the brokenness of being human. We all deal with the downward pull of temptation and the epidemic of error. When we succumb, it's all downhill from there.

The Downward Slide

My family likes to hike. A few times we've hiked a place called Stone Mountain that features the home of the world's biggest boulder.[4] That boulder is huge, standing 600 feet above the surrounding area. It's also smooth and rounded but then drops off almost imperceptibly. The guides at the visitor center say that before it was fenced off, people tried walking down the boulder. They found themselves sliding with nothing to grab. It wasn't as if they were falling off a cliff. They just slowly slid down, all the way down to their deaths.[5]

> "In our quest for real love and authenticity, we often ignore the ugliness that lurks in our own hearts."

The same happens with our own kryptonite. How many times have we said, "I know what I'm doing. I'm in control. I can get back up again"? But that is not what happens . . . not at all.

In our quest for real love and authenticity, we often ignore the ugliness that lurks in our own hearts. We don't want to admit that we struggle, or own up to our own selfishness when we want what we want when we want it. We don't want to confess that we have made decisions that have ended badly for us and for those we love.

But when we keep our struggles in the dark, they own us. If we don't come clean with our shady intentions, they pull us into the downward slide toward destruction.

And that's what happened to King David . . .

Wrong Place, Wrong Time, Wrong Decision

David became a warrior king with an established kingdom. He won many victories in battle and vigilantly protected Israel's borders. He was both feared and respected by leaders in the surrounding nations.

In those days, kings had a "war season," which was generally in the spring when mud wouldn't cause chariots to get stuck. During one war season, David decided to hang back in Jerusalem. This was a problem, because kings were supposed to fight with their troops. David was not supposed to be home sipping mai tais by the pool and starting his tan. He was supposed to be leading his troops, engaging in battle, confronting the enemy.

Around 50 years of age, David evidently decided to take a break and let the younger men go without him. Maybe he was thinking he deserved a little time off. Or he wanted to work on his songwriting. Maybe he wanted to study himself in the mirror and hum a little tune about how he was fearfully and wonderfully made. Maybe he was sampling the wine for the social season. Mostly, we know he was napping. History tells us that one day, late in the afternoon, David got up from his nap and went to the palace roof.

Archaeological digs reveal that the palaces of Israel's earliest kings were taller than any surrounding building. That means David could look down to see other rooftops or courtyards. While he was on the palace roof, he saw a beautiful woman bathing. She wasn't an exhibitionist. The baths were located on rooftops because the afternoon sun did the job that a hot water heater does now, 3,000 years later. David had a good vantage point to see her roof. Her house was close to the palace, where people of importance lived. The farther away you resided from the palace, the less prominent you were.

David didn't get embarrassed or cover his eyes. He didn't look away. Make no mistake about it, this was ancient porn. Far from looking away, he stared.

The thing about staring is that you steer where you stare. David started steering all his resources in this woman's direction. Staring is what moved David toward the side of the giant boulder that was straight down. Staring was what got David's downward slide started. That woman was David's kryptonite. Her name was Bathsheba.[6]

Focus ... Focus ... Focus ...

The principle is, you have to pay attention to what you are paying attention to. This isn't a riddle. It's a fact of life that helps anchor your life. When David saw Bathsheba, he could have taken different steps. He could have put up a wall to shield her and protect himself. He could have put a filter on his computer. He could have stopped going to that section of the palace roof. He could have gone back inside to have a quiet time just loving God. He could have gathered some of the mighty men who knew him and asked them to help hold him accountable. But instead he kept steering toward what he was staring at. And in that time of staring, new intentions developed. He walked straight off the edge.

David sent a messenger to find out who this beautiful Miss Israel contestant was. His people told him her name was Bathsheba. She was married. Her father was a well-known, influential man. And her husband, Uriah, was one of David's closest friends. (Wait, *what*—?) Yep, Uriah was one of David's mighty men who had fought alongside David for years.[7]

Yet David didn't let these facts deter him, as we like to think they would have. No, David kept staring. Indeed, his actions were wrong in every way.

What happened? Blinded by his kryptonite, David wasn't concerned about anyone except himself. That is the place where we usually make our worst mistakes. Worn out. Empty. Wanting. Trying to fill a void.

David doesn't plan on ruining his life or jeopardizing his country. He just wants a little time in the company of a beautiful woman.

A pleasant diversion after his nap. So he takes action. David has a messenger bring Bathsheba to the palace. Oops! He sleeps with her. Then he sends her home.

And that little sidestep is his undoing.

Good Intentions

Our decisions in life determine our destination. It is important to know the truth about the intentions of our hearts. Who knows what David was saying to himself? But inwardly, if he'd been honest, he knew his intentions were dishonorable. David's son would one day write this proverb: "People may be pure in their own eyes, but the Lord examines their motives."

Isn't it amazing how incredibly good and intelligent people can convince themselves that the wrong they are doing is "fine"? Why is this? It's because our intentions become the ingredients for action. When our intentions don't match up with our purpose in life, we just look at them through a different filter so we can justify our actions. And we can justify ourselves for *anything.* "I'll only have one" are the famous last words of every diet that ever died. "I'll go tomorrow" are the famous last words of every workout program that ever died.

We have to learn to weigh intentions against possible outcomes. Instead of asking ourselves, "What do I want right now and how can I get it?" we should ask ourselves, "Where will this decision likely put me?" This kind of prevention is a powerful tool against kryptonite.

The Hebrew word for prevention is *fuca,* spelled PUWQUH (which is why so many people flunk Hebrew). It means "a heavy conscience." Fuca makes us think about the consequences of our actions before we take action. It makes us sip the potential shame of the decision now, so we don't have to guzzle the regret later.

Fuca helps us say "no" to ourselves more often.

Yes and No

The two most powerful words in the English language are *yes* and *no*. The ways we use those words determine the decisions we make. And the decisions that we make eventually make us.

Every time we make a decision, we point our life in a certain direction. Show me a decision, and I'll show you a direction that you're about to head in. Pile up enough decisions in that same direction, and I'll show you your ultimate destination as well.

Just imagine that you want to go to Telluride to ski, but you have never been there. You don't start driving and say, "Gee, I hope I end up in Telluride." Why? Because you're not going to end up in Telluride by randomly driving.

You put the address into your GPS first, and then you start driving. You make a decision: "Yes, I'm going to Telluride" or "No, I'm not going to Telluride."

Making the decision ahead of time is your only hope of getting to the right place. It's true for driving. It's true for life.

Am I going to do drugs when my friends ask? Yes or no?

Am I going to sleep with this person I'm not married to? Yes or no?

Am I going to take things that aren't mine? Yes or no?

Am I going to talk about people in a negative way when others around me are gossiping? Yes or no?

Am I going to cheat on my spouse with someone who makes me feel good about myself? Yes or no? My good friend, Lysa TerKeurst urges us in her book, *The Best Yes* to use the two most powerful words, yes and no, with resounding assurance, graceful clarity, and guided power.

Tons of situations can cause us to slide down a boulder *if* we wait until we are in the middle of the situation *before* we decide what to do.

Error . . . Love's Opposite Day

Let's throw out all the petty rules of life and just keep anchored in God's love. When we are anchored in his love, it spills out on everyone around us. We make the best choices for ourselves and for those we love. Can't we all just do that?

No, sometimes kryptonite wins and we err. We act without love for God, for the people around us, even for ourselves. When we give in to the temptation offered by whatever kryptonite is glowing at us, it's the same as pressing a self-destruct button.

The pull of what we want rather than what is best and good and right unleashes a downward drop in our lives. It takes us out, and then we end up taking out the people we love, too.

The fallout from David's choice to sleep with Bathsheba was monumental. It wasn't just one mistake, one time. It was one error piled on another, piled on another, like a giant snowball, a giant slide, a cascade. Here's what it looked like:

1. **Lust**—David stared at Bathsheba and decided he wanted her. No matter what.

2. **Lying**—David lied to himself, justified his actions, and convinced himself that it was okay to hook up with his friend's wife.

3. **Manipulation**—David involved countless messengers to do his dirty work, first using them to get info about her and then to summon her to the palace. Sounds like Hollywood producers—kings—preying on aspiring actresses and young male actors just because they can. #Metoo, anyone?

4. **Betrayal**—David betrayed his friendship with his friend and fellow warrior, Uriah, by seducing his wife.

5. **Abuse of power**—When Bathsheba was summoned to the palace, she didn't have much choice.

6. **Adultery**—David slept with Bathsheba.

And now, for the rest of the story. Bathsheba became pregnant. That must have taken guts for her to tell him. When she told him, he instantly thought what any adulterer would think—*cover up!* Not very fatherly. And absolutely no acceptance of responsibility. He started a huge cover-up operation in hopes that Uriah would never find out. But David had a huge problem. Uriah wasn't home and hadn't been home for a while because Uriah was fighting the war that David was supposed to be fighting. So here's where his bad decisions start piling on:

1. **Deception**—David brought Uriah home from the front, in the guise of checking on him and asking how the war was going. He hoped that Uriah would sleep with Bathsheba.

2. **Coercion**—Uriah was too honorable to sleep in his comfortable bed when his soldiers were still at war. He refused to go home, so David got him drunk. But not drunk enough to go home. Uriah was resolute about not taking advantage of being summoned by the king. He slept in front of the palace.

3. **Conspiracy to commit murder**—Desperate, David started conspiring. He told his nephew Joab, the leader of the army, to place Uriah in the worst part of the battle and leave him, to ensure Uriah would be killed in battle. This may be the low point of the whole sick story . . . David had Uriah himself carry his own death sentence to Joab!

4. **Disloyalty**—David betrayed the loyalty of his men, who served under him willingly, by making them unwitting accomplices in murder.

5. **Murder**—Uriah was thrust into the worst part of the battle and killed.

6. **Mass murder**—Other warriors were killed with Uriah.

7. **Theft**—Bathsheba went into mourning when she heard that Uriah was dead. After the mourning period was over, David brought Bathsheba to the palace and married her.

All told, David stole Uriah's life, and then he stole Uriah's wife.

David, once described as "a man after God's own heart," was now a liar, adulterer, manipulator, murderer, and then mass murderer. He was sucked so deep into error that for this short season of his life, he had no heart at all. He thought of no one but himself.

How Could This Happen?

You're probably thinking, *How could this even happen to such a great guy?* But . . . really? I often find myself doing stupid things, don't you? Before we check out and say, *Nah, that could never happen to me*, let's just think about silly mistakes that happen because we're not really paying attention. Maybe one thing led to another, and pretty soon you found yourself in bizarro world. I'll tell you one of my most ridiculous mistakes.

I enjoy officiating at weddings. Some are pretty big. Some, like for special friends, seem especially romantic. One Saturday we had both when a dear friend planned a huge outdoor wedding on a warm day in June. My wife left early to ensure every design was exactly as the bride had wanted. I stayed home to prepare for the ceremony.

After a couple of hours that included prayer, I felt great, prepared, happy for the couple. I closed the little wedding journal I use during ceremonies and headed to my bathroom. As the shower water warmed up, I snapped off the guard of my razor and trimmed my sideburns. Checked them—even, perfect. I jumped into the shower and probably sang the best I'd ever sung. I jumped out, toweled the steamy mirror a little, and grabbed my razor again.

Somewhere in my family, a very hairy person's genes left me with bushy eyebrows. Let me guess—you just flipped to the bio picture on the inside book cover jacket to see the unibrow freak. Am I right? I trim them with a razor that has a safety guard to keep my brows at a certain length. In fact, to keep them neat, I run the razor over them most days. Very routine. On this day, the mirror was still steamy, but I grabbed the razor and, from memory, pressed it across one eyebrow. Still not seeing anything more than a vague outline of my face in the foggy mirror, I pressed it across the other brow. As I set the razor back on my sink, I saw the safety guard—the thing that keeps the hair at a certain length so I can't shave the hair clean off. The safety guard I had removed before my shower. *THE GUARD!*

My bare hands flew to the mirror and rubbed furiously to let me see myself. As I drew them back, I looked at the mirror and into an eyebrow-less face. My brows were shaved right down to the skin. Both sides. No brows.

Not wishing to make a fashion statement on the most important day of this couple's lives, and really not wanting to have to see their pictures later, I called my wife. She told me where her eyebrow pencil was and explained by phone how to make eyebrows, drawing one hair at a time. I did it. Not bad. But then I knew I was going to sweat in the summer air. So, I went back to my wedding journal and wrote in big block letters on every page: DTE. It stood for "don't touch eyebrows." And I didn't.

Hardly comparable, I know—but don't miss the point. I wasn't paying attention to routine things, and one of those routine things went south on me. Today I have a funny story to tell because of it. And I never trimmed my eyebrows so flippantly again. These little incidents can wake you up and help you course correct before they become *big* incidents.

Cruise control was what David's life was on for far too long. For far too long he was just mailing it in and taking nearly everything in life for granted. Just scrolling through the ancient Instagram feeds of others until one caught his eye. For me, I was just taking my morning routine for granted and sleepwalking through getting ready for the biggest day in this young couple's life. David had been sleepwalking for months! Drifting away from God for months. Bored out of his mind for months. Losing his bearing for months. I'm fully convinced he had no idea how far he'd drifted. By the time he'd committed the worst sins of his life, he was miles and miles and miles from home.

Because with that in mind, we can continue with David's story of the most contemptible thing he ever did. And perhaps we can understand a bit more how easy it is to start stepping slowly down a wrong path and end up sliding all the way to the bottom.

David Sees Himself in a Mirror of Sorts

As good as his heart was, David must have known right from wrong. Out of love for God and for others, he had certainly made preemptive decisions about moral issues. But there's one more thing we need to do besides making preemptive decisions about our intentions. We need to stay close to God and trust him to guide our hearts.

David wasn't living out the purpose that God had shown him to fulfill. David was drifting. When we don't stay anchored to God's love, we drift. The power of the drift away from God can come as a bit of a shock, especially when we realize what we've done. The records of King David's reign are clear—what he did was pure evil.

But God still loved David. He didn't let that evil slide. He didn't let David self-destruct. He helped David get honest with himself. Real quick.

God told a prophet named Nathan to confront David. Pretty nervy, but Nathan knew his purpose, and there was no way he was going to screw it up. So Nathan went to the king with a completely fake but optically powerful story he made up about a horrible situation in the kingdom. I picture them sitting on sumptuous cushions across from each other, drinking aromatic tea.

Nathan tells his tale. "A rich man had tons of money and plenty of sheep. A poor neighbor had only one little sheep. He loved that sheep so much that he raised it with his children as part of the family. When a traveler arrived at the rich man's house, instead of killing one of his own sheep to prepare a feast, the rich man called for the poor man's beloved lamb. He got it, killed it, and ate it."[8] David flies up off his cushion, outraged. How did this rich guy think he could get away with such callous evil? David calls in an officer and demands that he find the rich man and put him to death. But Nathan springs to his feet, thrusts a finger in David's face, and shouts, "YOU ARE THAT MAN!"

David crumbles back into his cushion. Yes, he sees it. He was the rich man with everything. Uriah was the poor man with nothing but his beloved Bathsheba.

Nathan doesn't let up. He thunders, "Why did you despise God and do evil in his sight? You have killed Uriah with the sword and taken his wife *to be* your wife."

He drops onto David's cushion, where the king's face is buried in his hands. Now calm, Nathan lays out the consequences that God had told him. "Your Highness, God says the sword will never depart from your house, because you have despised God by what you did." He says David's neighbors will one day sleep with David's wives in public, as retribution for what David did in secret. And then he breaks David's heart. He says the baby Bathsheba is carrying won't live.

Crushed in his heart, David gets honest with himself. He sees the enormous wreckage that his "little sidestep" has unleashed. He will have to live with the consequences for the rest of his life. He pulls his hands from his face, looks up at Nathan, and makes one of the greatest understatements in history: "I have sinned against the Lord."

Then Nathan gives him a message of hope: "God has put away your sin. You won't die."

God despises people who say they love him but purposely, consciously, do the opposite of their life purpose. In a way, they're saying they "despise" what God wants for them, what God does for them. And yet, the God of love, who can't stand to look on such evil, forgave David the moment David got honest.

The weird thing? God does the same for us. Not all of us are going to be big important kings or push forward the wheels of world history, but that doesn't matter to God. God loves us *just as much as* he loved David. How can that be? It just is. It's crazy love.

So, what do we do when we make that ridiculously stupid, inane, asinine, half-witted, brainless, ill-advised, uneducated, mindless, senseless loser move? We own it. We get gut honest with God. We change our behavior. And then God forgives us and gives us hope. Hope for reconciliation. Hope for the future. Hope for a healed heart.

Honesty Shmonesty

As we learn about love and authenticity, most people find it hard at first to be honest with others, or with ourselves. If we want to be real with ourselves and with those we love, we have to admit when we struggle. We have to confess that we have kryptonite and are about to take a trip to Vegas and snowball out of control.

It wouldn't have done much good for me to walk out the door and officiate at a wedding pretending I had eyebrows. That wasn't going to cut it. Neither does it do a whole lot of good to ignore any of our problems. When we lie to ourselves about our areas of weakness, our kryptonite, we open ourselves up for failure. Just like the nuns. Just like David. We are just like them. Human.

What we need to learn is how to prevent this kind of life-ruining sin from taking hold in our hearts in the first place. We do this by crowding it out of our hearts by putting in something else—the healing, hope-filled words God had people write down for us. God's truth about who we are, and who he is, keeps us anchored in his love and forgiveness.

> **"When we lie to ourselves about our areas of weakness, our kryptonite, we open ourselves up for failure."**

Many of the words of King David's songs were recorded in history. We can still read them. In one lyric he says, "Your word have I hidden in my heart that I might not sin against you!"[9] Sounds as if he'd learned a painful lesson.

Read God's words. That will help you stop making mistakes and start making good decisions.

David learned that God in his love has mercy for us. He loves us unconditionally. Even when we are deaf to his commands. His plan for us is to give us hope and a future. A new start means being surefooted, not sliding. We can kiss Vegas good-bye, because if we listen continually to God's direction, we won't be tempted to head there in the first place.

When we lose the optics and get honest with ourselves and with God, when we anchor ourselves in his truth, a love journey with him paves the way for real, authentic, grace-filled relationships—with others and, most importantly, with ourselves.

And that is a worthwhile journey. Let's get going.

A CHANGE OF HEART

When we succumb to the downward pull of temptation, we self-destruct. When we anchor ourselves in God's love, everyone wins.

THINK

- We tend to give in to our weaknesses during the times in life when we think life, God, our family, or our job is somehow ripping us off.
- We don't usually take a giant plunge into bad decision-making, but one tiny sidestep leads to another tiny sidestep until we veer off the path completely.
- We steer where we stare. Our decisions in life determine our destination.
- *Fuca* makes us think about the consequences of our actions before we act.
- When we are anchored in God's love, we make the best choices for ourselves and for those we love.
- God has a message of hope and forgiveness for us, despite our past sins and failures.

PAUSE

- How can you put *fuca* (a heavy conscience) to work for you?
- Thinking about your recent decisions, in what direction are you pointing your life?

- We have all experienced the fallout from bad decisions. How has this fallout impacted the way you view others and their struggles?

- God offers you hope for a healed heart and reconciliation. How does that change how you view your future?

CONNECT

The Lord is compassionate and merciful, slow to get angry and filled with unfailing love. He will not constantly accuse us, nor remain angry forever. He does not punish us for all our sins; he does not deal harshly with us, as we deserve. For his unfailing love toward those who fear him is as great as the height of the heavens above the earth. (Psalm 103:8–11, NLT)

RESPOND

God, you know that I struggle with temptation. Give me the strength that I need in my moments of weakness. Forgive me for the ways that I haven't loved you and others. Heal the hearts of those I have wounded with my poor choices. Please help me to become the person you created me to be. Thank you for your unfailing love and forgiveness. Amen.

Chapter 8

The Love Test

A century ago, a professor of comparative literature at Sarah Lawrence College named Joseph Campbell saw common threads in stories across different cultures.[1] With years of study under his belt, he developed a plotline called "the hero's journey."[2] It's the story that all of humanity is drawn to. The hero encounters different phases, like the call to adventure, meeting the mentor, engaging enemies and allies, and overcoming huge tests, ultimately conquering his fears and triumphing in the end. (Cue *Star Wars* anthem!)

George Lucas used Campbell's pattern for his space myth, *Star Wars*. In it, Luke Skywalker gets a call to adventure by seeing Princess Leia's call for help through R2-D2's technology. (*Help me, Obi-Wan Kenobi. You're my only hope.*) He joins forces with Obi-Wan and his allies, Han Solo and Chewbacca. (*We love you, Millennium Falcon.*) He finds his purpose when he joins the rebellion and becomes a fighter pilot to rid the universe of evil.[3]

It's hard not to geek out about *Star Wars*. But Luke didn't come into his own until he was tested. His failures and triumphs shaped the hero that he was becoming. He wrestled with anger, doubt, and fear. He faced his enemy, Darth Vader, who wanted him to embrace the dark side and rule the empire, but he finally triumphed when he used the good of the force. #intergalacticdaddyissues

Star Wars broke the box office when it came out.[4] More than 40 years later, we still love Luke's journey. We are invested. We want good to triumph over evil. We still want to see the destruction of the evil empire. (*May the force be with you.*)

With any good storyline, the hero has to overcome conflict. It is what makes a story interesting and allows the hero to grow and change. The funny thing is, in our own hero's journey, we would rather not face conflict or grow or change because it's not comfortable or easy. And as brave as we try to tell ourselves that we are, we are all naturally drawn to comfortable and easy. We want to become the person we are destined to be without the stress, confusion, and struggle of real life.

When we start loving God and others, we expect it to be easy. We think life just got easier. *I'm a big kid now. I'm lovin' it.* We have been programmed for certain expectations, so we are super surprised when the road we are walking becomes unpredictable and difficult.

If we are being honest and authentic, life is almost never perfect. Especially not when we are finding our purpose in life. But God uses the tools of life and the trials of life to chisel away at our character and to make us more real and authentic, like him.

> "But God uses the tools of life and the trials of life to chisel away at our character and to make us more real and authentic, like him."

What Image?

In our journey of life, God is shaping our hearts with love, transforming us like David into men and women who have hearts like his. That is the image he is going for, while most of us are caught up in trying to achieve an image of perfection.

In our hero's journey, one of the first struggles we face has nothing to do with perfection. It has to do with us allowing God to reveal our imperfections, hopefully not as dramatically as he had to do for David. God lets our issues deal with us before we have to deal with our issues.

We have to recognize that God's got a purpose for us, even when life doesn't look or feel as we think it should. We have to go head-to-head with temptation and face down the urge to do it our own way.

Authenticity and Authority

In *Star Wars,* the rebellion is a good thing. They are a group of scrappy heroes who are wielding their power against the evil empire. But in real life, "rebellion" works against us when we follow our own hearts and take what we want when we want it. That's how David ended up murdering Bathsheba's husband. But it's also more than that. Pride comes in when we think we know better than God. We forget to follow his lead, and we take over.

We come by our prideful, rebellious natures honestly. Our culture honors the rule breakers and the rebellious. We don't have to look far to see it. We are a culture of individuals. We value the individual over the group, and we really don't like authority. We're taught from every voice, from the media to our universities, to buck authority. Get creative. Find a new way. Stick it to the man! We tend to worship our own opinions. And we don't submit to anyone, if we can help it.

Many of our celebrities, sports figures, journalists, university professors, political figures, and others who are often the most popular in our culture are remarkably rebellious. We value that, thinking they are cool, and we sometimes want to emulate them.

Sometimes the individualistic attitude works out for us. Fred Smith famously received a C on a college paper that laid out his plans for FedEx.[5] Undaunted, he left school and started a company that changed all of shipping. Most of the time, we need the wisdom of others in order to succeed. It's pride that says we can do it all and have it all on our own terms. We're not generally interested in anyone telling us what to do . . . even God. But if we want God to lead us on our journey, we have to start with humility. That's rough. None of us are naturally gifted in humility, and those who are are pretty proud of it. But God only uses people who are humble enough to accept his authority.

David wasn't perfect when God anointed him, but he was completely available to God, and that made him a perfect match. Swipe right. What God wanted for David, David wanted for himself. God doesn't choose glittery jars to pour his love into. He chooses flesh and blood, regular people with open lives that he can fill with purpose.

Humility recognizes that God is the ultimate authority in our lives. David got this. Because without God, David knew he couldn't do much. The thing is, if we think we can achieve the perfect life without God, we're basically useless. May as well just keep promoting your avatar, pretending to be a superhero, and trying to collect "likes" for the rest of our lives. But it's not nearly as satisfying.

When David was anointed king, he gave his storyline to God. He just wasn't quite prepared for how crazy his life was going to get. In the decade following David leaving Jonathan and fleeing Saul,

David went through one nightmare after another. He was a refugee in his own country, running and hiding for his life. He left behind friends and family for years. He lived in caves. In foreign nations. People whom he loved turned against him, telling him he wasn't qualified to be king.

And what was God doing? Why wasn't he doing a better job of taking care of David? Wasn't David the chosen and anointed one?

God's not looking at those optics. Through a process of trials, God was chiseling David's heart. Samuel had anointed David as king, but David wasn't prepared to be king. He had a lot of growing to do. God took off the rough edges to prepare him so David could have a hugely successful reign. God didn't want David to lose that heart that beat like God's own heart. God

> **"Humility recognizes that God is the ultimate authority in our lives."**

wanted to develop and foster the trust that David had in him so God could make him one of the greatest leaders in world history.

God was testing David's love for him, and that test ended up strengthening that love. I'm no King David, and yet because God loves me, he's given me a few moments like that in my own life.

My Teen Years Test

In high school, my Big Head Small Body life took a slightly better turn. Dodgeball was out. Drama was in. Music was in. Dancing was in. My body was finally proportioned, and I found out it was more than a little coordinated. That Big Head Little Body boy had also grown confidence. I was pursuing a close relationship with God and held a firm belief that God had a purpose for my life. Life was good. Almost.

An announcement came out that a big production of *West Side Story* would be coming to my high school to commemorate the class musical's 10-year anniversary. *Get the beat, Jets!* Legendary composer Leonard Bernstein wrote the score, and Bill Meyers directed the Broadway version of it at our school. Bill earlier became famous for his work with the great crooner Johnny Mathis. Unbelievably, Bill accepted the role to direct this anniversary production *at my high school.* The community was abuzz. School leaders were agog. It was a tremendous honor, a big deal. And I inserted myself right into the middle of this huge event. Yes, Big Head Small Body decided to audition for the lead male role, Tony, the "Romeo" in this retelling of the Romeo and Juliet story.

At this time, if anyone had taken a peek at my optics, they would have said no way. I was holding my own for acting and singing onstage, but behind the curtain, my home life was beyond crazy. I found the relationship between my parents stressful, and for all sorts of reasons, our family moved 22 times before I was 19. Around this time, another relocation was in the works as my father eyed a new job in Chicago, and I didn't want to go. I had things I wanted to pursue, and I was hopeful about them. But I remember my father telling me he didn't think I had a hope or prayer of getting the part, and with that, the choice to move was made.

In spite of everything, I auditioned. And I got the role. Unreal. This was the chance of my teenaged lifetime. But now I had to figure out how a God-seeking teenager was supposed to act like a creepy gang member on the stage. I guess I had a mouth on me even back then, because everyone in my school knew that I was part of Young Life, a group of students who wanted an authentic relationship with God. People knew I didn't drink or get involved in anything that would negatively affect my witness for God. Even at that age, I was completely focused. I wanted my life to fulfill God's purpose.

As a result, I wasn't sure about acting the role as it was portrayed in the Broadway version, which was a little edgy, even trashy. I didn't want to act one way onstage and be another way offstage. It was perhaps my first real crisis with the whole authenticity, avatar, fake-life, optics thing. I decided to tell the director, Bill Meyers, about my dilemma. His words were just as encouraging as my father's. He dismissed me by saying, "We don't need you. I'll give your role to the understudy."

I left the theater heartbroken. My father's insults kept rolling around in my head. The uncertainty of his move also left me wavering. Feeling desperate, I tried to figure out where my true Father in Heaven was in all of this. *God, why is this happening?* Finally, I just prayed. I said, "God, if you're the one who gave me the honor of playing this role, then I'm asking you to keep me in it. Please don't let me be overlooked just because I am standing up for what I believe is right. Please change people's minds, especially Bill Meyers', and tell them to let me play the part in a way that honors you. But if you don't want me to do this, I won't. Whatever you want God."

The craziest thing happened. God went all Opposite Day.

The highly respected, perfectionist director Bill Meyers *came to me* and apologized. He said he was sorry *to a high school kid.* He said, "I was wrong. You were our first choice for the role. We really need you to make this production special for the anniversary. But I need you to make a deal with me. You come in and give the lines, and if you do well, you can do the—as you call it—'more honoring version.' Deal?" I agreed. And I gave the play my all. I worked hard, playing gang member Tony in the most God-honoring way I could. Acting in that play was one of the greatest thrills of my early life, and for the closing months of my senior year and beyond, it opened the door for even more conversations about Jesus with fellow students and teachers alike.

What was such a big deal, and proved to be a big hit, is now a faded memory. But what God built into my heart through that experience has never faded. And that's the point—that's exactly why we have those rough spots. God used the hard moments, the scary situations, to shape my heart. I couldn't change my dad. I couldn't change Bill Meyers's mind. I couldn't smooth out my parents' relationship. I couldn't arrange my life the way I wanted it to go or even soften the painful optics so many were starting to see. But I *could* surrender myself to God. I *could* trust his love. I *could* humble myself to believe that he was on my side. I *could* rely on him to come through for me.

And he did. I'm no David, but he came through for Big Head Little Body, just like he did for David in the wilderness. *Just think of what he'll do for you!*

> **"God used the hard moments, the scary situations, to shape my heart."**

As you become your authentic self through God's love, you will be put to many tests. Following, I will describe these tests—of arrogance, authority, advantage, and association.

I've used David as the example. His tests are a little more life-and-death than my own. (I wouldn't have *died* if I couldn't play Tony. I just would have been disappointed. And this book would have had a big blank spot.)

The Arrogance Test

A drama unfolded from the moment David stepped up to challenge Goliath. His first test was the *arrogance test*. When David showed up on the battlefield with a delivery of biscuits for his brothers, he already knew that he was God's anointed and he was going to be king. But he didn't flaunt that. When he decided to fight Goliath, he went to King Saul, the leader, and asked permission. Saul was as encouraging as my dad. He said, "You're too small to fight him."

David didn't get mad or rebellious. Instead, he made a righteous appeal. He said, "But the Lord's been with me. I've killed lions and bears that came against the flock of sheep that I have. He's been with me, and he'll be with me again." Because of David's humility, Saul changed his mind. (That, and nobody else stepped up to fight Goliath. So . . .)

David knew his love relationship with God. He trusted God's purpose for his life. He accepted it without arrogance, secure in knowing that God would help him face Goliath.

The Authority Test

The second test David faced was the *authority test.* When David moved into the royal palace, King Saul was already struggling with jealousy. The first time Saul chucked a spear at David, David moved out. When conditions got better, David moved back in. This happened a few times, meaning that Saul had numerous opportunities to explore his own heart and make it right with God. But Saul wouldn't, didn't, and refused each chance he was given. Finally, Jonathan helped David get out of Saul's path for good.

Here's what David did when he left. He didn't dishonor Saul. He didn't gossip. He didn't go around telling everyone, "Listen, this guy's lost it. He's nuts. Let's get a rebellion going and storm the palace." David trusted God to remove Saul from his position of authority in God's own way and God's own time. Until he did, David honored Saul as his leader and king.

The Advantage Test

The third test that David faced was the *advantage test*. God has a peculiar way of allowing our actions to come back around to us. Saul experienced that during an awkward moment with David that revealed to him his own jealousy and hatred.

As David wandered in the wilderness, a band of men started following him. Most of them were also running for one reason or another. One by one their hearts were moved toward God like David's. Together, they became friends and allies, with David as their leader. People around the country called them the "mighty men." For years on the run they lived by their wits, hiding in caves, sustained by the kindness of those who supported David and by the mighty hand of God. Infuriated by the same old grudge, jealousy, and fear, Saul tried to catch up with the band so he could get rid of David. Some people never learn.

One day while Saul was hunting David, nature called. Saul went into a cave to relieve himself. What he didn't know was that David and his men were hiding farther back in the exact same cave. David had the advantage over Saul. But Saul, thinking he was alone in a private place, went about doing his business. #awkwardmoment

Perhaps on a dare from his men, or due to a whimsical moment of his own, or even because of a nudge from God, David snuck up behind King Saul with his knife. He could have killed him, but instead he cut off a piece of Saul's coat. Saul finished his bio break, gathered up his garments, and left the cave. Once Saul was beyond the range of a spear, David emerged from the mouth of the cave.

"Hey there!" he yelled, waving the piece of fabric in the air. "Missing something?" Saul and his men turned. Incredulous? Embarrassed? David went on, "Some of my men told me to kill you, but I didn't. I told them I would never harm the king because you were God's choice."

In perhaps Saul's best moment, one that proved he had at least a little heart, he shouted back to David, "You are a better man than I am. You repaid evil with good. You have been amazingly kind to me today. You could have killed me, but you didn't."[6]

What would you do if you were abused, threatened, and mistreated, and then God placed the abuser's fate in your hands? And what if your abuser was your *in-law*? (If you happen to be married, you might know where I'm going here.) A whole lot of us would opt for revenge. It's natural to desire justification, but David knew better than to seek revenge on his own terms. He knew God's job. He knew his job. Saul's fate was above his pay grade. He stayed in his lane. He didn't take advantage of a situation, no matter how much he may have wanted to.

The Association Test

The fourth test David faced was the *association test*. While David ran and hid, life elsewhere went on. Saul, Jonathan, and the army kept fighting the Philistines. Their final battle did not go well. Saul and three sons, including Jonathan, went down.[7]

As the Philistines were closing in, Saul lay dying, blood oozing out of him. He said, "Somebody just kill me so my enemies won't torture me!" His men wouldn't kill him, so history says Saul "fell on his sword." The Philistines found him dead, then cut off his head and started to party.

A man from the neighboring nation of Amalek raced to deliver the news to David. He tore his clothes and put dirt on his face as if he were mourning. He took some of Saul's possessions to show David and thought, *I'm going to be a millionaire.* Then in triumph, he told David that his archenemy was dead and that he, the Amalekite, had killed him.

David saw it a little differently. He thought, *Why would a foreigner who worshiped idols dare to lay hands on a leader chosen by the one true God?* David asked, "Why were you not afraid to kill the king appointed by God?" By that point, the Amalekite was probably rethinking his position and starting to sweat. There was nowhere to run.

David told one of his men to kill him, then turned to the man and said, "You have condemned yourself with your own words. For you confessed that you killed the Lord's anointed one." Then David led his men in mourning for the deaths of Saul and Jonathan. He refused to associate with someone who had gone against God.

In the middle of facing test after test, David stayed connected with God. Although Saul had come against David many times, David didn't let himself get caught up with hatred, bitterness, or even resentment. He didn't even rejoice that his own ordeal was finally over. He chose to focus on the fact that great warriors who had protected Israel for years had fallen. He was no faker. He didn't have to act as if he was mourning. He mourned.

How David lived his life up to this point shows us that understanding and accepting authority accelerates spiritual understanding and maturity. When David faced obstacles, he grew and matured.

The Love Journey

With each test God gave, David proved he would keep trusting and loving God. God also used those difficult moments to prove to

David that he was trustworthy. He had David's back. Since David's time, millions upon millions of people have gone through and passed the same testing. Some have achieved greatness on their journey, and some even fame. We already talked about the tremendous test passed by Elisabeth Elliot. Here are a few more who made history:

DR. DAVID LIVINGSTONE

Growing up in a poverty-stricken family, David Livingstone worked in the cotton mills as a child, then put himself through medical school.[8] After graduating, he went to Africa on an antislavery campaign as a doctor-missionary. His goal was to help Africans avoid slavery by finding trade options. Africans loved him, and even though David was no preacher, thousands of Africans accepted his God and his crazy love as their own. He blazed the way for more missionaries, not only by exploring and mapping routes but also by showing how to share God's love in tangible ways.

ERIC LIDDELL

Eric Liddell was born in China to missionary parents.[9] When he attended school in London, he found his gift for track. He earned a place on the team for the 1924 Olympics but dropped out of the 100-meter final because the race was held on Sunday, which he felt was a sacred day for God. But he went on to win gold in the 400. A movie was made about his track career, called *Chariots of Fire*. What people don't know is that he returned to China and dedicated himself to them. When China was overrun by the Japanese during World War II, he was captured and died in captivity.

HUDSON TAYLOR

Hudson Taylor was determined to take God's love to the people of China, which at the time meant enduring a six-month boat trip just to get there.[10] He was one of the first European missionaries to adopt the local customs where he went. He grew his hair into a long queue, adopted Chinese clothes, and learned many Chinese dialects. His legacy paved the way for hundreds of workers to pour into China, and his example changed many entitled Westerners to adopt respect for other nations. Taylor left behind many inspiring statements, including this one: "All God's giants have been weak men who did great things for God because they reckoned on him being with them."[11]

Your Love Journey

Your hero's journey is not going to look anything like David's. Or Hudson Taylor's. Or Eric Liddell's. Or David Livingstone's. Or mine, for that matter, so skip the dance lessons. Your epic journey will most likely be filled with both challenges and joy. It will be different— difficult and beautiful all at the same time.

Best of all, it will be real. It won't be pretending. It won't be fake. It will be filled with real love and authentic relationships. And in those dark times, when you think God is nowhere around, he's always there . . .

A CHANGE OF HEART

God uses the trials of life to make us more real and authentic, like him.

THINK

- We want to become the person we are destined to be without the stress, confusion, and struggle of real life.

- Our culture honors the rule breakers and the rebellious, not the humble. Humility recognizes that we are not in charge.

- God is shaping our hearts with love and lets our issues deal with us before we have to deal with our issues.

- In our hero's journey, we become our authentic selves through the tests God allows in our lives.

PAUSE

- Humility recognizes that God is the ultimate authority in our lives. How do you trust God's authority in difficult situations?

- What would you do if you were abused, threatened, and mistreated, then God placed the abuser's fate in your hands?

- How are you achieving maturity during times of testing in your life?

CONNECT

And yet, O Lord, you are our Father. We are the clay, and you are the potter. We all are formed by your hand. (Isaiah 64:8, NLT)

RESPOND

God, I know that you have a plan and purpose for me. I know that you want me to mature as I face trials and struggles in life. I humble myself before you. You are the one who is in authority. You are in charge of my life, not me. Help me to trust you and surrender my heart completely to your timing. Thank you for working in my life and shaping my heart to look like yours. Thank you for your unfailing love.

Chapter 9

Love in the Valleys and Caves

The Colorado Rocky Mountains have 54 or 58 peaks that surpass the 14,000-feet mark (depending on whom you ask). Mountaineers call these "fourteeners."[1] More than 300,000 people summit these mountains annually. Andrew Hamilton is the superhero of Colorado's "fourteeners club."[2] In July of 2015, at the age of 40, Hamilton traversed all 58 peaks in a mind-blowing 9 days, 21 hours, and 51 minutes. He set a new world record for the quickest consecutive ascent, supported by family and friends who repacked his gear, cooked his meals, and cheered him on.[3] I enjoy a challenging hike, but this is pretty over-the-top. This guy must have quads of steel.

There is something addictive about pushing yourself beyond your limits and climbing to the top of a mountain. The funny thing about mountaintops is that you can't stay up there long. Even in the summer, it's cold up there. You hike up to the summit. You take your picture. Then you go back down. Done. And if you're Andrew, it's repeat, repeat, repeat.

The truth is, most of us spend most of our time not on a mountain but in a valley. It's true physically and also spiritually.

Hero in the Valley

David knew a lot about valley life. He'd been tagged as Israel's future king, but getting there was rough. Mountaintop victories were elusive. He went from hero to zero and back to hero in, oh, about 15 or 20 years. There was no quick summit for him. When David started running through the wilderness to get away from Saul, his life was in constant danger. Quite often, he didn't even know where he would get his next meal. Hardly the optics one would expect for a future king. Shouldn't there have been lessons a king would need in deportment, manners, and diplomacy? Didn't happen.

The wilderness was a rough-and-tumble place, and it's still a rough place for us today. In a culture that believes only health, wealth, and overall prosperity could ever equal God's love, what do we do when we enter the wilderness? Does this mean God has forgotten us? Is he there for everyone else but not for us?

There must have been plenty of moments when David was crouched in a cave, hungry and cold, thinking, *Is this what God meant when he said he wanted me to be king? Really?*

David was about to give up.

Doubt, Fear, and DNF

In the world of marathon running, DNF means Did Not Finish.[4] Sometimes after months of training and perseverance, participants don't finish the 26.2 miles they set out to conquer. Illness, injury, or even a faulty mindset can cause a runner to pull out of a competition. Taking a DNF is cruelly disappointing. It can destroy a runner's confidence for future races, as doubt creeps in about being able to achieve the goal. Marathoners can get stuck. For David in the wilderness, it was as if he was stuck mid-marathon, floundering in a dark place of doubt and fear. A DNF was right around the corner.

David likened his wilderness to a long and difficult valley. He wrote a famous song known as "The Twenty-Third Psalm." In it, he proclaims, "Though I walk through the valley of the shadow of death, I will fear no evil. . . ."[5] What is interesting is that he sang about going *through* the valley. He understood something extremely important: God doesn't just call us *to* the valley; he calls us *through* it!

> **"David may have forgotten for a while that the valley is a process to get through, not a place to live in."**

David may have forgotten for a while that the valley is a process to get through, not a place to live in. Often, our tough moments in the valley can paralyze us. We stop instead of taking the next step with God. Our minds begin to wander from the truth of God's love. We look at our life and think, *I love God and I gave everything to him. But the optics of my life make it seem as if he doesn't love me.* Those thoughts begin the downward spiral into the dark.

David's DNF

Spiritual doubt is part of most valleys. But how did it creep into David's mind? Time after time, God had protected David as he was on the run. David had fully trusted God to rescue him from Saul. After escaping from Saul in the cave, David said, "Let God judge which of us is right and punish the guilty one. He's the one who will rescue me from your power." Another time, he said, "God will reward me for being faithful. He will rescue me from trouble."

For Saul's part, he had left David at the cave but then did an about-face and began hunting David again. At that point, something shifted in David. He got marathon tired. Some call it "war-weary." In his exhaustion, David's thoughts gave way to fear. History records that he thought, *Someday Saul is gonna get me.* At that point, fear gave way to doubt.

David began to doubt his purpose. Even worse, he doubted God. This thrust David into his greatest test. If he was going to fulfill his future as a king, he was going to have to overcome his own doubt and fear.

Three Kinds of Doubt

Doubting for David started the same way it does for all of us. With a thought. We encounter three types of doubt on our hero's journey.

INTELLECTUAL DOUBT

Intellectual doubt creeps in when it seems as though what God has whispered to us is inconsistent with our human experience. We haven't experienced it, so we can't believe it. When we read about God's miracles, we think, *That must have been myth or legend, and if God's word is not true in those instances, then maybe it's not true for me, either.* We allow doubt to hit our pause button. People say it "gives us pause." Everything stops. When we pause, we don't pass. When we stop, we don't take next steps.

MORAL DOUBT

Moral doubt moves in when we don't like God's commands or when following the path he's given us seems too difficult. We rationalize our doubt. We think, *I guess I don't believe in God or his word after all.* This is a convenient way of relieving guilt or escaping accountability. David never stopped believing in God altogether, but his doubt took him deeper and deeper into the valley. That meant further and further from the comfort of God's unending love.

CIRCUMSTANTIAL DOUBT

Circumstantial doubt comes when we go through a long period of difficulty. Adversity wears on us. The lawsuit drags out. The spread of illness doesn't stop. The school year stretches on. The friends are still mad. Relief never comes. We begin to doubt that God is in control of the circumstances. If he was, we figure, this wouldn't be happening.

For nearly a decade, David lived the life of a fugitive, constantly in danger, escaping death day in and day out. Eventually, he succumbed to feeling sorry for himself. After all, he was innocent. He had spared Saul's life. Didn't he deserve better? Where was God? Why didn't he do something?

David had repeatedly witnessed God's protection, but now he thought that maybe God had given up on him. He let what he thought were rational thoughts trump love. His love was shaken. He'd shaken loose from his hold on God.

> "To make it to the end of the marathon, we have to attach ourselves to God's love and truth."

Haven't we all experienced moments of deep and often depressing doubt? At times, we come up against difficulty or adversity and reach for a quick boost instead of tying ourselves to the truth of God's love. We tend to detour into addictions, wrong friendships, or the pseudo-friendships of social media. To make it to the end of the marathon, we have to attach ourselves to God's love and truth. It's the only way to the end of the race. The way out of the valley.

Dodging Defection

Doubt left unchecked in our hearts can cause us to defect. As so often happens when anyone gives up on God, David made a major mistake. He *defected* to the enemy camp.

Once David started dwelling on the first negative thought, *Someday Saul's gonna get me,* he descended into more negative thoughts. He shifted from thinking, *God will always protect me* to *I'm going to die. I can't depend on God, so I'll take matters into my own hands.* He decided to go where Saul *wasn't*—to the cities of Saul's and Israel's archenemies, the Philistines.[6] *Then I'll be safe,* he thought.

David's doubt led to a separation from God's love, which led to a lack of dependence on God. From there, David descended into defection from God and his people. At this point, his thinking was so twisted David thought that hanging out with Goliath's family and friends was his best bet. How did that go?

"Hi, I'm David."

"Hi, I'm Boliath. You may know my Uncle Goliath."

"I sort of remember that name. What's he look like?"

"He's about nine foot nine, muscular, wears a lot of bronze."

"Nah, never saw him. I was thinking of some other guy."

What kind of crazy is it when David believes that he is safest among his nation's enemies? Among the friends of the guys he killed? Vacationing in the enemy camp doesn't usually end well.

Focus ... Focus ... Focus ... Again

Motivational speaker Zig Ziglar called David's negative mindset "stinkin' thinkin'." Zig said we need "a daily checkup from the neck up" to stay in the right frame of mind.[7] Anytime we emphasize and verbalize the negatives in our lives, we are headed for trouble. When we dwell on our problems, we are done for.

I've experienced this often mentally, but I learned it physically from mountain biking. I love biking, but you have to remember to focus on the trail ahead or you can get hurt. I have proven this to be true. If there's an obstacle in your way, you're not supposed to look at it for too long. You can't let your mind dwell on it. You have to pull yourself together, get your eyes back on the trail, and *focus*.

Twice, I wiped out just because I focused on the obstacles in front of me instead of the trail ahead. The first time, I came up on a narrow tree pass with a few inches of clearance on either side. I started focusing on the tree to my right, thinking, *I don't know if I can make it.* As I focused on it, I ran right into it, flipped over my handlebars, and dislo-

> **"When we dwell on our problems and make them the focus of our lives, we take God and his steadfast love out of the equation."**

cated my shoulder. We talked earlier, in David's rooftop story, about the truism "You steer where you stare." I stared my way into a sling.

The second time I crashed, it was into a huge boulder in the middle of the trail. Seriously! In the middle of the stinking trail! With a straight shot of about 50 yards to consider it. Never was something easier to miss! I had been on this particular trail before. I knew the boulder was there, and I knew where it was. As I approached the area, I started thinking, *I do not want to hit that. I do not want to hit that. I do not want to hit that.*

There was a clear path to the left and to the right, so bikers had options. All you had to do was choose one or the other. But that day, all I could think was *That's a big boulder, and I'm coming up on it pretty fast.* I hit it square on. Why? Because *I was dwelling on the rock, not on the road.* My foolish focus created a gravitational pull stronger than the largest black hole.

Have your experiences been similar to mine? Are you constantly thinking about bad optics? Are you pessimistic or critical? Is your negativity spilling over into your behavior? You might be in the process of defecting from God.

We have to *think about* what we are *thinking about.* When we dwell on our problems and make them the focus of our lives, we take God and his steadfast love out of the equation. When we defect from God, we never get out of the valley. We never leave the wilderness to do the great things that God has planned for us.

We have to shift our focus to the trail ahead. We have to lock on to the purpose that God has for us and the love he surrounds us with. We have to never let go. It is not his intention for us to *stay* in the valley, just to *learn* in the valley. David finally realized this.

Deliverance

In a moment of clarity, David woke up one morning and packed up to leave the Philistines. He finally had his confidence back. Instead of focusing on his problems, he started telling himself the truth. Several truths, to be precise.

- Saul is not my master. He's just a man.
- This wilderness I've been in for so long is not my home. That must be somewhere else.

- God called me to be king. I need to start acting like one.

- Maybe this is my training ground, and God's trying to chisel off the rough edges of my life that don't look kinglike.

- Maybe when I start looking and acting like a king, I'll be a king.

- The Lord hasn't forgotten me. He's just preparing me.

- I wasn't called *to* this place. I was called *through* this place.

David returned to being the confident man "after God's own heart." When he would eventually become king, he had a lock on truth. God didn't *desert* David in the wilderness; he *developed* him in the wilderness.

David learned he could trust God even "in the valley of the shadow of death." David would face this valley more than once. Doubt and fear have a way of cropping up throughout our lives.

- One time, the Amalekites ransacked David's camp, stealing away the women and children.[8] David's own men turned on him and wanted to kill him. (Harsh!) David found strength in his God.

- David later fought the surrounding nations. He relied on God and his direction.

- Untimely deaths, "the sword," continually plagued David and his household. This was what Nathan the prophet said would be the result of his sin with Bathsheba. Over and over again, David reached for and worshiped the God who sustained him by his grace and mercy.

> **"God didn't *desert* David in the wilderness; he *developed* him in the wilderness."**

- When his own son, Absalom, turned against him and tried to overthrow his authority, David knew that his anointing came from God alone.[9] David's life-giving relationship with God anchored him for the rest of his life. That's where God is taking you today.

The Truth in Our Valley

God wants to develop you, just as he did David. You will experience different kinds of valleys from David's, and from mine. By entering your valleys with the same attitude David learned to cling to, with the same mindset David learned to adopt, you can change the outcome of every valley. Instead of dread, you can expect to get fed. Instead of fearing that God is going to burn you, you can trust that he is going to teach you. God loves you. He has a purpose for you. You can trust him, no matter what.

Here's an idea. Instead of fearing what God might do in our lives and instead of dreading the tools he might use, what if we started *chasing* the chisel? He wants to smooth the rough edges of our hearts, so what if we let him? What if we pursued his refining power? When we recognize the refining of the Lord, we don't just have to endure it; we can celebrate it. God is shaping us in his image. It's called "dying to yourself." It means you give up, at least temporarily, all your own plans, all your own thoughts, and you just lean back and say, "Here I am. Teach me."

Jesus's half brother James wrote, "Count it all joy when you fall into various temptations, knowing that the testing of your faith produces endurance. Let endurance have its perfect work, that you may be perfect and complete, lacking in nothing."[10] The valleys are made *for* us. They're not working *against* us. We don't have to be afraid of valleys. That's where God crafts us, chisels off the rough edges, teaches us new thought patterns, and expands the limits of our endurance. It's where we learn we can go the distance, run the marathon, climb the mountain, and achieve everything God planned for us from the moment of our birth.

On your hero's journey, you get to be *you*. You don't have to "fake it till you make it." You get to have valleys, and God will walk through them *with* you. You don't have to be a superhero; you get to be the real *you*.

A CHANGE OF HEART

Mountaintop experiences may be few and far between, but the valley is a process to get through . . . not a place to live in.

THINK

- Most of us spend our time not on a mountaintop but in a valley. Spiritual doubt is part of most of life's valleys.

- We experience circumstantial doubt, wondering if God is in charge, when adversity strikes.

- We can detour into addictions, wrong friendships, or the pseudo-friendships of social media when we doubt the goodness of God's love.

- Anytime we emphasize and verbalize the negatives in our lives, we are headed for trouble. Pessimism and complaining can lead us to defect from God.

- Lock on to the purpose that God has for us and the love he surrounds us with. Instead of dread in the valley, expect to get fed.

- Tell yourself the truth about who you are and who God is.

PAUSE

- Have you experienced a "DNF" (Did Not Finish) in your life? How has it affected your decision-making?

- Do you experience "stinkin' thinkin'" in the middle of adversity? How can praise and gratitude shift your doubtful attitude in difficult times?

- How has God developed you in the "wilderness" or "valley" of life? How has he fed you?

- What does it mean to be the "authentic" you in times of difficulty?

- What would it look like if you "chased the chisel" in your life?

CONNECT

Dear brothers and sisters, when troubles of any kind come your way, consider it an opportunity for great joy. For you know that when your faith is tested, your endurance has a chance to grow. So let it grow, for when your endurance is fully developed, you will be perfect and complete, needing nothing. (James 1:2–4, NLT)

RESPOND

God, I admit that sometimes I doubt you and your ways. I don't always understand why you allow certain circumstances into my life. I need you to help me change my perspective. Replace my doubt with belief in your goodness and the knowledge that you love me, no matter what is going on in my life. Help me get through the valley I'm in. Thank you for your care and provision in my life. Amen.

Chapter 10

Superheroes and Sacrifice

Karen was an unlikely superhero. She was a funny, bright 37-year-old who loved spending her summers traveling. She liked baking lemon bars and going to the movies. Her nine-to-five job was working as a detention officer in the Bakersfield County jail. But her heart was more about setting people free.

In 2003, she took a leave of absence from her job at the jail. She sold her house and her car. She loaded all of her worldly possessions into a duffel bag. Then Karen hugged her family and friends, dropped off a letter at her church, and boarded a plane for Iraq. She felt God was calling her to show the Iraqi people his unconditional love for them. God had shaped her heart for a purpose. Karen had learned that clean water could revolutionize a village, so she was going to do relief work. She wanted to bring hope and health to communities by bringing in a mobile water purification plant.

A year later, on a relief trip to Mosul, someone shot and killed Karen and two fellow workers in a drive-by shooting. At the news of her death, her family and colleagues were rocked with grief. The pastor at her church opened the letter she had given him, with instructions that he only open it if she died.

Karen's letter began with "When God calls, there are no regrets. To suffer was expected. His glory is my reward."[1]

Like Jim and Elisabeth Elliot, David Livingstone, and so many others before her, Karen's heart and life had been transformed by God's love. Overflowing with love, she wanted to share God's love with others. She was a picture of that love when she sacrificed her own life.

You can't get much more "real" than that.

Life's Great Themes

Turn on any good movie, and you will experience one of three main themes: love, hope, and sacrifice. For any of these themes to enter the picture in any meaningful way, they have to be preceded by hurt and pain. Seriously, ever notice how the greatest stories always hurt? I checked. Not a single one of the 100 top-grossing movies of all time were comedies. I love a good comedy, but they're hardly life changing. They seldom tug at the heart. They aren't meant to. But in the hero's journey, the greatest plotlines always move us, and they always hurt.

In *Avengers: Endgame*, the moment of raw sacrifice is when Black Widow and Hawkeye fight for the honor to sacrifice their life for each other. By doing so, they will attain the Soul Stone and save the universe. A soul for a soul. They cling to the side of the cliff, Hawkeye gripping the Black Widow's wrist. She says with deep love, "Let me go." Kicking off from the side of the precipice, she plunges to her death. Her soul for the souls of millions. (I'm not crying. *You're* crying.)

The Big S, sacrifice, is the most powerful plotline of all. Deep down, the theme of self-sacrifice strikes a chord in each of us. For someone to give their own life for another is an unpleasant beauty to experience. The horror of death is sprayed with the fragrance of supreme love. Jesus is recorded as saying, "No greater love has a person than this, that they would lay down their life for their friends."

Karen went a step further than laying down her life for her friends. She left her friends, abandoned the comforts of her home, and laid her life down for people she didn't even know. She didn't go to take selfies: *"Look at me, how I'm helping Iraqis!"* In our narcissistic, selfie-happy, look-at-me world, Karen was looking at someone else. She was thinking of someone else. She was loving someone else. God. God's son. Jesus.

Son of David

When David became king of Israel, Nathan told him that God was making a covenant with him: "I will be his father, and he will be my son. I will correct him like any good father would, but I won't take my favor away from him like I did with Saul. Even better, David's heirs will continue on the throne forever."[2]

God made good on his word when, 14 generations later, Jesus was born to David's heir, Joseph, in a love match that was never consummated—as Mary was a virgin when she gave birth to him. (In case you never noticed, it's why we sing at Christmas, "Silent night, holy night . . . Round yon virgin mother and child.")

Jesus, who was also called the "Son of David," was nothing like the superheroes we love and admire today. Historians say he didn't hang out with the cool kids, the rich, or the powerful. He was the last person anyone would think would be king. At one point, someone scoffed about his hometown, "Has anything good come out of Nazareth?"[3] Nazareth basically had the same reputation as Liverpool before four shaggy-headed musical geniuses made history by sweeping the world with their tunes. But here came Jesus, bursting onto the scene, with a ragtag bunch of guys that no one thought twice about. Like David, he was gathering his own group of "mighty men," and also like David, he couldn't have cared less about the optics.

Jesus was never politically correct. He was an equal-opportunity irritator, dissing religious leaders and annoying the government. Jesus only cared about one thing: connecting people (you and me) to God. Period. Got one? Good. Repeat. Got another one? Great. Repeat. These were "real" followers, people whose hearts were transformed by coming into contact with Jesus, not just thumbs-up and heart emojis.

Jesus's birth and life became the fulfillment of over 300 ancient prophecies. He didn't come to earth as a mere man like his great-great-great (etc.) great-grandpa David. And he wasn't just a "good man" or a "man after God's own heart." He was God on earth. Jesus was and is the ultimate hero. He is a flawless, perfect, omniscient (all-knowing), omnipresent (everywhere at once), omnipotent (all-powerful) being . . . the true God.

> "A life centered around the love of Jesus is the only way to have the life that we long for and the life we are made for."

Movies often elevate humanity above God. (Narcissists!) But a life centered around the love of Jesus is the only way to have the life that we long for and the life we are made for. And in this crazy world, we need Jesus and everything he gives us. Hope. Peace. Joy. Friendship. Loyalty. Honesty. Forgiveness. Faithfulness.

Jesus gives us all the things we are looking for in our own lives and in our authentic relationships. He has already done everything necessary to give us all of this. It's just that a lot of us haven't made that connection yet.

The Real Connection

When Jesus was on earth, he didn't go about making people "perfect." He didn't create his own "image." He didn't teach coping skills to troubled people. He didn't filter the difficult parts of life. He spoke truth, lived truth, taught truth, and walked around as truth personified. He ripped the two religious parties—the Pharisees and Sadducees. He called them "whitewashed tombs," saying they might look good on the outside, but they were dead on the inside. He could have been talking about influencers or social media addicts today. He could have been talking about Republicans or Democrats. He could have been talking about me.

Who wants to get in the way of *those* words? Ouch! But Jesus talked that way because he *loved* people. And he loves us today. He even loves people who have made him their enemy! He loves the mess-ups, outcasts, and untouchables. He came to spring people out of their fake, addicted, and troubled lives and set them *free*.

Hope at the Well

One outcast whose life he reached was a woman from the hated Samaritan ethnic group. Jesus met her at a well in the middle of the day, during the highest heat.[4] She was most likely there to avoid meeting up with most people, who came when it was cool. She was a Samaritan, hated by Jews, and a woman with a bad reputation, hated by her own Samaritan people. Harsh.

Jesus saw something different in her, something that others

didn't see. He saw a woman longing for real connection. So he reached out to her and said, "Give me a drink."

When Jesus asked her for a drink, he didn't really need her help to get a drink. This was Jesus. He was with God creating lakes and oceans. He was with Moses parting the Red Sea. And his first miracle was to turn water to wine. No, he didn't need help with a beverage.

Jesus asked her for water because he wanted to draw her focus to her own dry condition. He wanted her to see her parched life, her own thirst, and all the dead-end ways she tried to satisfy that thirst.

She responded, "I don't have a bucket." Jesus explained that he had living water he could give her. He said that if she drank it, she would never thirst again. Jesus had her attention. She said she would really, really like some of that "living water."

She admitted her need, but she was really saying, "Please help me so I don't have to be trapped. I don't want to keep sneaking back here and hiding. I don't want to have to keep performing. I don't want to be so mad and angry. I don't want to keep being so . . . *thirsty* for life. I want *real* life."

The woman was in a trap of her own making, caused by her own choices and her attempts to correct those choices through the wrong means. She was dying for an authentic connection with someone who really loved her. Until that moment, she had lost hope.

Jesus said, "Okay, go get your husband."

Then she admitted another need: "I have no husband."

Then Jesus shook her. He said, "You are right when you say you have no husband. The fact is, you have had five husbands, and the man you are living with now is not your husband."

She was probably thinking, *Have you been following me on Instagram?* Or maybe, *Stalker!*

"Sir," the woman said, "I can see that you are a prophet." But no. He is not a prophet. He has just revealed that he is the Messiah. He is the Savior all of Israel has been hoping for.

This man who acknowledges her knows every detail about her hurting heart and ugly past. She is stuck in a trap. Jesus sees her for who she is *and* for who he made her to be. He affirms her worth. Only Jesus, who cannot be trapped, can set trapped people free.

In that moment, the woman *believes*. Her thirst for being known and loved is quenched. This woman is no longer ashamed of herself. She no longer feels the need to hide from people. Instead, she runs back and tells everyone in her village, "Come and meet the man who told me everything I ever did. Could he be the Messiah?"

The village outcast became the village evangelist. This is what hope looks like.

Forgotten Battle

Japanese soldier Lieutenant Hiroo Onoda had lost sight of hope. During World War II, he had been sent to the Philippines as an intelligence officer to help thwart an Allied invasion in 1944. His commanding officer told him, "We'll come back for you. No matter what."

When the war ended in 1945, Hiroo took to the hills with a band of soldiers. They hid in the jungle. When leaflets were dropped, telling them the war was over, they didn't believe it. Hiroo was waiting for his commanding officer to come back and get him. He waited 29 years. He didn't get picked up.[5]

So many of us today are waiting for something that already happened. We're fighting a battle in a war that has already been won. We have all lost hope at times. We see the miserable state of things,

> **"The truth is that everything you are looking for in this life, in your relationships, in finding your purpose, is already available to you."**

the racial tensions, people living in poverty around the world, genocide, greed, and hatred. It paints a picture so dark and tangled we sometimes can't get God's message of love through Jesus.

The truth is that everything you are looking for in this life, in your relationships, in finding your purpose, is already available to you. Like the woman at the well, we all have hope for a new way of living. By sacrificing his life for ours, Jesus won the war against selfishness, against loneliness, and against fear.

Love, Hope, and Sacrifice

Real hope, like the woman at the well found, is seldom offered outside of love. And the greatest love is never cheap. Rescue for all humankind is about a whole lot more than self-redemption—it takes a sacrifice equal to the task. It takes a sinless, perfect sacrifice.

Jesus found himself surrounded by enemies, the religious leaders of the day. He was deserted by his followers and friends.[6] Jesus was put through six mock trials in one night for a crime he never committed. He was beaten, scorned, and ridiculed as the government officers blindfolded him and put a crown of thorns on his head. As blood poured down his face, they beat him so badly he was unrecognizable. Then they nailed him to a cross.[7] As he was bleeding out, officers gambled for his clothes. The religious leaders mocked him, saying, "Look, he saved others, but can he save himself?"

But here is the thing. Jesus saw the trouble the world was in, sin-sick, broken, hurting, longing for real relationship. Jesus looked at his Father and said, "Let me go."

Instead of letting us die, sin-sick and trapped, Jesus offered up his perfect life in place of our imperfections. Not a soul for a soul. *The* soul for all souls. For all of eternity.

Why? Because he couldn't stand to see us doing life alone. We were made for life with him, for life-giving connection with God, and for our hearts to be full of love for others.

At sports events and on billboards, you'll commonly see signs emblazoned with John 3:16. That's the reference for the mission statement Jesus had when he came to earth. It is "God loved the world, so he gave his one and only son, Jesus, so that everyone who believes in him will not perish but have eternal life."[8]

God loves us with such outrageous, crazy love that he was willing to send his son, Jesus, to earth to save us. On that cross, Jesus looks not just at his surroundings but at all of humanity. In the midst of his pain, he says, "Father, forgive them. They don't really know what they're doing."[9]

Jesus gave up everything to have a real connection with us and lead us into an authentic relationship with God. Jesus is looking to quench our thirst, to fill us to overflowing with living water. He wants to set us free from our wanting, our hurting, and our endless grasping. He wants to free us from what is fake and inauthentic and from the things that entice and entrap us.

> "Jesus is putting you on a path where you don't have to be 'liked,' because you are really, truly, and wholly *loved*."

The good news for you and me today is that the battle is over. All the grasping and posing is over. Jesus knows everything you ever did. He still affirms you. He knows where you are now and what you do in private. He loves you and wants to free you from shame. And he knows what God intends for your future.

He's putting you on a path where you don't have to be "liked," because you are really, truly, and wholly *loved*.

And we all know which is not only more important but also vital.

Your Hero's Journey

So now it's your turn to live a life with no regrets.

You are God's masterpiece. Seeing yourself as God sees you means looking at the value he places on you for the beauty inside of you.

You have value because of who *he* is, not because of what you look like, what you do for a living, who you know, what car you drive, or how expensive your shoes are.

Seeing yourself as God sees you is actually giving praise to him, because it means you see the beauty in his most precious creation . . . you!

When you look in the mirror, what you see looking back is a daughter or son of the king eternal. You are a child of the king. Made in the image of God himself.

You were made for authenticity. You were made for wholeness. You were made for true relationship. You were made to unleash God's amazing, crazy love on the world around you.

Don't wait. Get going.

A CHANGE OF HEART

Everything that you are looking for in this life, in your relationships, in finding your purpose, is already available to you through the hope of Jesus and his sacrifice.

THINK

- The theme of self-sacrifice strikes a chord in each of us. The horror of death is sprayed with the fragrance of supreme love.

- Jesus is the ultimate hero. He is a flawless, perfect, omniscient, omnipresent, omnipotent being . . . the true God.

- Jesus loves the mess-ups and came to spring people out of their fake, addicted, and troubled lives and set them *free*.

- We were made for life with him, for life-giving connection with God, and for our hearts to be full of love for others.

- You are God's masterpiece. Seeing yourself as God sees you means looking at the value he places on you, based on your true inner beauty.

PAUSE

- Have you ever sacrificed something for someone else? What was your motivation?

- Have you ever been caught in a trap of your own making? What did that feel like?

- *You were made for authenticity. You were made for wholeness. You were made for true relationship. You are made in God's image.* How do these truths impact your view of yourself?

- Jesus gave up everything to have a real connection with us and lead us into an authentic relationship with God. If you have made the choice to connect with God, how has it changed your life?

- When we let him take charge of our heart, soul, and mind, our lives take on a singular focus. Just as David's did. When God is at the center of our lives, the deepness of his love for us calls us to experience it even more on an even deeper and greater level. We never get bored when our eyes remain on him.

- When we strain to follow him, our heart is filled with joy and purpose and love. When we fix our eyes on him, we will receive the one thing our soul truly longs for: himself.

CONNECT

For this is how God loved the world: He gave his one and only Son, so that everyone who believes in him will not perish but have eternal life. God sent his Son into the world not to judge the world, but to save the world through him. (John 3:16–17, NLT)

RESPOND

Perhaps you are thinking, *I don't have any idea what it means to be a son or daughter of the king. I haven't asked Jesus to be in charge of my life. I don't really even know what that means.* Don't worry. You can do that right now. A relationship with Jesus, God's Son, is what you are designed for. It is the whole reason Jesus came to earth. The most beautiful gift ever purchased and the most important decision we ever make is accepting the forgiveness and salvation that were bought for you and me on the cross.

It would be the worst tragedy if you finished this book and tried to apply some formulas for addiction-free, victorious living without embracing God's love for you and his forgiveness for your sins. There's no easy formula for this. Rather, it's all about giving your heart to Jesus and then pressing into that commitment with your heart every day for the rest of your life. It's about loving God and loving people. These actions make for a victorious life.

If you're ready to ask Jesus into your heart, to receive his forgiveness, and to be adopted as a son or a daughter of the living king, you can pray silently in your heart right now. You just talk to God as David did.

If you don't know what to say, you can say this prayer:

Father, thank you for sending your son, Jesus. Lord Jesus, thank you for giving your life on the cross for me. I'm sorry for the things I've done wrong. I am admitting right now before you that I'm a sinner.

But God, I know you don't mean to leave me that way. I'm unqualified. But I want to be qualified in you. I want to do great things. I receive your forgiveness purchased on the cross. And I invite you to come into my heart right now and be my Lord and be my Savior.

I don't understand it much right now, but I feel your presence, and I believe you're here. So I commit to you. From now on, you are the one who will be in control of my life from this day forward. Thank you for your crazy, outrageous love for me. I'm excited about my new life in you. In Jesus's name. Amen

Conclusion

The Love Reboot

Augustine was focused on his self-centered life. Raised by a God-fearing mother and a pagan dad, loving God and others was just about the last thing on his list. His dad's style fit him more. As soon as he was able, he left home to fulfill his heart's greatest desires. A Roman citizen and philosopher, he was looking for success and prestige. He wanted "followers."

He was a social climber and a player when it came to the ladies. Fear of what others would think of him kept him from marrying his longtime concubine, the mother of his son. She was of a lower class. It would have ruined his optics.

The problem was, good optics or not, Augustine felt empty inside. He was ruled by his passions. He struggled with good choices. He kept switching philosophies. He was confused and desperate. He wasn't the man he wanted to be. He said, "I looked for pleasure, beauty, and truth not in him but in myself and his other creatures, and the search led me instead to pain, confusion, and error."

Polished for a Purpose

Narcissism, fake relationships, and self-centered choices hadn't brought him the fulfillment he had longed for. It's funny, isn't it, that even though Augustine lived in 300 AD, his problems sound very much like problems many of us face today?

One night, Augustine experienced the crazy love of Jesus. He felt compelled to pick up the apostle Paul's letter to the Romans, which is part of our Christian Bible. It read, "Because we belong to the day, we must live decent lives for all to see. Don't participate in the darkness of wild parties and drunkenness, or in sexual promiscuity and immoral living, or in quarreling and jealousy. Instead, clothe yourself with the presence of the Lord Jesus Christ. And don't let yourself think about ways to indulge your evil desires."

Those words pinned Augustine to the wall. Paul's words seemed to apply directly to him. Wild parties? Casual sex? Drunkenness? Those were his go-tos.

> **"To fall in love with God is the greatest romance; to seek Him the greatest adventure; to find Him, the greatest human achievement."**
>
> —SAINT AUGUSTINE OF HIPPO

But Jesus loved Augustine (just as he loves you). He had more for Augustine than shallow relationships and self-centered living. He wanted to shape Augustine in his image.

Like the woman at the well, Jesus was inviting Augustine to live a different life—a life full of hope and love. Jesus cracked Augustine's heart wide open in what was actually an agape intervention, drawing on the type of love that is unconditional and divine. Augustine changed into a man "after God's own heart." God helped him go Opposite Day on the optics.

Augustine's life shifted from self-focused to God-centered. He described his change of heart, saying, "To fall in love with God is the greatest romance; to seek Him the greatest adventure; to find Him, the greatest human achievement."

Saint Augustine of Hippo went through a love reboot. That love relationship with God and others spilled over into his life's work. He was a changed man. He went from being a party boy in pursuit of followers to a God-lover pursuing authentic connection with God and others.

Saint Augustine's writings still shape Christian life to this day. His was definitely a life repurposed by love.

Reboot, Repeal, Replace

Like Augustine, we have a unique opportunity for a love reboot. God commands us to love him and love others. Why do you think that is? Because we are made for love.

Love is not just a feeling, as we've seen. Love is an action. When we move into a new season of loving God and others, we will make a commitment to recenter our lives around him instead of ourselves.

As a marriage counselor, I see the effect that inaction has on relationships. In the busyness of life, people get disconnected. Their relationships unravel. They come into my office and are so far apart it's like they are sitting on the world's largest sofa. The distance between them is physical and emotional until I start asking them questions. You can see their minds start to filter back through those times of connection. They start remembering the fun and the joy. They start telling the story of how they met and fell in love. And before you know it, they're sitting close to each other. The world's biggest couch becomes a love seat. It is a love reboot. Love takes action. Intentional time spent together. Serving each other. Hanging out. These moments of togetherness solidify the bonds between spouses.

Our relationship with God is no different. Love requires action. We are wholly loved by God. Because of that, we respond to him, spend time with him, and talk to him. We read his words of love. Those actions are what solidify our relationship

Battleplan for Defeating Selfitis

Disclaimer: I need to be brutally honest with you here. This isn't going to be easy. Nothing worth doing ever is. But if you approach this like kicking the tires at a used car dealership, you won't make it. Better to approach it like Tom Cruise's character, Ethan Hunt, in the *Mission Impossible* movies.

At the start of each movie there is the familiar challenge issued from the IMF (Impossible Missions Force). As the challenge is issued, it doesn't take long to comprehend that the mission being set forth is not for the faint of heart. Therefore, a choice to accept or reject is always made, and it goes something like this: "This is your mission, should you choose to accept it." The choice is offered only after the mission and consequences have been carefully laid out.

If you are a Christ follower reading this, you need to know that 2,000 years ago, right before Jesus ascended into heaven, he left his followers with what must have sounded like a heavenly version of a directive from the IMF. It's found in Matthew 28:16–20: "Then the eleven disciples went to Galilee, to the mountain where Jesus had told them to go. When they saw him, they worshiped him; but some doubted. Then Jesus came to them and said, 'All authority in heaven and on earth has been given to me. Therefore go and make disciples of all nations, baptizing them in the name of the Father and of the Son and of the Holy Spirit, and teaching them to obey everything I have commanded you. And surely I am with you always, to the very end of the age.'" This is the greatest IMF challenge ever issued—even earning the moniker "The *Great* Commission." And there is none more important because this one comes from God himself.

If that in and of itself isn't enough to motivate you, consider the words of the great apologist and theologian C. S. Lewis in his book *Mere Christianity.*

"Creatures are not born with desires unless satisfaction for those desires exists. A baby feels hunger; well, there is such a thing as food. A duckling wants to swim; well, there is such a thing as water. Men feel sexual desire; well, there is such a thing as sex. If I find in myself a desire which no experience in this world can satisfy, the most probable explanation is that I was made for another world."

Put another way, if changing the optics of your life over and over again is not filling that longing inside for something more, then that longing cannot be satisfied cosmetically. You must move beyond the optics.

It's my hope and prayer that I've laid out thoroughly not only the challenge of chasing after "likes" and other forms of approval for validation but also the consequences of taking it all too lightly

> "If changing the optics of your life over and over again is not filling that longing inside for something more, than that longing cannot be satisfied cosmetically. You must move beyond the optics."

and trusting your eternity to chance. The stakes could not possibly be any higher. So consider the choice set before you and then . . .

Choose.

But choose wisely.

This book will self-destruct in 15 seconds!

First, Devote 21 Days

Scientists tell us habits can be changed in just 21 days. Likewise, in a mere three weeks—21 days—we can do a love reboot. We can turn down the volume of social media and turn up the volume in our relationship with God and the people around us. As God surrounds us with his love, we get to respond with action. As our hearts begin to change, our actions overflow to those around us.

We replace the negative thoughts and actions with positive thoughts and actions. Each day becomes an opportunity to cement an authentic connection. Each action solidifies the love relationship we have with God. The love that is shaping and polishing us.

We will start the reboot with a prep, to help us succeed in our commitment. Each day will repeal a negative action and replace it with a positive action.

Remember that social media is neutral. It is how you *use* it that impacts your life. Think of this reboot as a relaunch of using your social media powers for good—to encourage, uplift, and tell the truth about who God is and who you are.

Treat this is an experiment, which means it doesn't have to go perfectly. Some actions may work great for you, others not so much. That's okay. Stick with it. Commit to love God and your people and see how your heart begins to change as you oust the pull of "likes" for the power of real connection and authentic love in the next three weeks.

Reboot Prep:

1. The first step in your reboot is to find a reboot partner or partners. Partnering with someone gives you an advantage.

2. Plan how and when you will check in with them each day. Use FaceTime, text, Marco Polo, or Snapchat to encourage each other with calls and texts.

3. Plan to meet with your partner one day a week to laugh and pray together. A face-to-face connection is a powerful encouragement.

4. Let your social media contacts know that you will be taking a break from social media in different ways for the next three weeks. This will help you be accountable.

5. Have your Bible ready. Pick a translation you understand and believe in. I recommend NIV or NLT. Your Bible is your go-to as you learn about how much God loves you.

6. Have a journal, a Google doc, or a voice recorder app to record your thoughts and prayers at the end of each day.

7. Make a playlist of your favorite worship songs to listen to throughout the day.

8. Check out several uplifting books from the library or download them on your reader. During those times when the siren song of social media is beckoning, you can choose to read instead.

Week 1 Scripture Focus

Read this psalm every morning and night the first week to reset your thought patterns.

Psalm 23 (NLT)

1 The Lord is my shepherd;
I have all that I need.
2 He lets me rest in green meadows;
he leads me beside peaceful streams.
3 He renews my strength.
He guides me along right paths,
bringing honor to his name.
4 Even when I walk
through the darkest valley,
I will not be afraid,
for you are close beside me.
Your rod and your staff
protect and comfort me.
5 You prepare a feast for me
in the presence of my enemies.
You honor me by anointing my head with oil.
My cup overflows with blessings.
6 Surely your goodness and unfailing love
will pursue me
all the days of my life,
and I will live in the house of the Lord
forever.

Week 1: Turn Down the Volume

DAY 1

- **Repeal:** Turn off all social media notifications on your phone and computer. Unhook yourself from the dopamine hits of "likes" and "thumbs-ups." This first day will be rough, but you can do it!

- **Replace:** Write Psalm 23 in the notes on your phone. Each time you want to check a social media app, read Psalm 23 instead. Use this any time throughout Week 1 that you need to refocus your attention.

- **Journal thought:** How do you feel that God is speaking to you through Psalm 23?

DAY 2

- **Repeal:** Swap out your normal Spotify playlist for your new worship playlist. Note any songs that encourage you.

- **Replace:** Every time you want to check your social media, hit play on your playlist.

- **Journal thought:** What does worship mean to you? What are different ways you can connect to God with worship throughout the day?

DAY 3

- **Repeal:** Do a quick mental check. Is there a social media app that leaves you feeling anxious and brings worry crashing in? Uninstall it for a day, a week, or even the whole reboot.

- **Replace:** Put the worship song that encourages you on repeat. Learn the words, and sing it throughout the day. (If you don't like to sing, just hum it to yourself.) Reframe those anxious thoughts with thoughts of praise.

- **Journal thought:** What about social media triggers your anxious thought patterns? How can you change its impact?

DAY 4

- **Repeal:** Disengage from news outlets for the day. Decide not to check headlines or engage in commenting on news stories.

- **Replace:** Find an uplifting Bible-based podcast and take time to be encouraged with truth and hope.
  (https://www.crosswalk.com/faith/spiritual-life/crosswalk-s-top-20-christian-podcasts-everyone-should-know-about.html)

- **Journal thought:** How does your intake of information impact your frame of mind? How can you best guard your heart and mind when it comes to information overload?

DAY 5

- **Repeal:** Disengage from Reddit or other online forums that you usually engage in.

- **Replace:** Have a text or email discussion about Psalm 23 with your reboot partner. What do you connect with in the psalm? What is a challenge for you?

- **Journal thought:** Write or record an entry about the verse in Psalm 23 that impacts you the most.

DAY 6

- **Repeal:** Put taking selfies on the shelf.

- **Replace:** Shift your focus by asking to take a picture of a friend or family member. Text them the picture along with an affirmation about why you like them.

- **Journal thought:** How much of your thought life is taken up by thinking of yourself? What are some ways you can shift your thoughts to God and others?

DAY 7

- **Repeal:** Do a full social media fast today.

- **Replace:** Go on a phone-free walk with your reboot partner or a friend. Discuss what you are learning in the reboot and what has been difficult or positive so far. Encourage each other.

- **Journal thought:** What are you noticing about your addiction to social media? What actions are helping you feel less anxious and more connected with God and with others?

Week 2: Scripture Focus

To reset your thought patterns, read this portion of scripture every morning and night during the second week.

Psalm 139:13–18 (NLT)

13 For you created my inmost being;

you knit me together in my mother's womb.

14 I praise you because I am fearfully and
wonderfully made;

your works are wonderful,

I know that full well.

15 My frame was not hidden from you

when I was made in the secret place,

when I was woven together in the depths of
the earth.

16 Your eyes saw my unformed body;

all the days ordained for me were written
in your book

before one of them came to be.

17 How precious to me are your
thoughts, God!

How vast is the sum of them!

18 Were I to count them,

they would outnumber the grains of sand—

when I awake, I am still with you.

DAY 8

- **Repeal:** Take a break from comparison and log off of Instagram and Facebook for the day. Comparison often triggers negative thoughts and feelings.

- **Replace:** Write or copy/paste this week's scripture focus in the notes from your phone. Use it as a replacement for checking your Instagram and Facebook.

- **Journal thought:** Focus on verse 14. What character traits or talents do you see that God has gifted you with? How can you praise God for making you fearfully and wonderfully?

DAY 9

- **Repeal:** Put interruptions on hold by either turning off or silencing your phone today. Check your personal emails only at the beginning and end of the day.

- **Replace:** Start a conversation with God. Throughout the day, instead of checking your emails or texts, tell him what you are struggling with or what you are enjoying. Invite him into the details of your day.

- **Journal thought:** After reading your scripture focus, spend some time (5–10 minutes) actively listening for the Holy Spirit. Do you have any thoughts or impressions about how God feels about you as his child and creation? Record these impressions.

DAY 10

- **Repeal:** Think about the "like" or "thumbs-up" emoji. These are shorthand for your approval. Don't add to your friends' likes or emojis today. Do something different.

- **Replace:** If you actually enjoyed a friend's post today, take time to think about them as a person whom God loves and created. Instead of adding your "like" to their post, DM them or text them and connect.

- **Journal thought:** God goes out of his way to connect with you and the rest of his kids. When you are connected and encourage his kids, you are loving him. What are different ways that you can love those around you and encourage them?

DAY 11

- **Repeal:** Leave your phone in your kitchen when you go to bed. Don't check it first thing when you wake up.

- **Replace:** When you wake up, start your morning phoneless. Get ready for the day without other people's agendas and thoughts barging into your mind. Give yourself time and space to connect with God through the scripture reading, and start your day by talking to him.

- **Journal thought:** Hearing from God (reading the Bible) and talking to him (praying) reshape your daily outlook. What kind of intentional step can you take today to carve out space for your relationship with God in the weeks ahead?

DAY 12

- **Repeal:** Shrug off narcissistic tendencies by thinking about and praying for others.

- **Replace:** As you read through your social media feed, do you notice anyone struggling with illness, family issues, or work trouble? Take a moment to pray for them by name. Use your feed as today's daily prayer list.

- **Journal thought:** When you take time to pray for God's kids, he responds. Write or record the names of those you prayed for today. Write the date next to it. Note how God responds to these prayers.

DAY 13

- **Repeal:** Resist the urge of checking in with celebrity gossip sites or reading celebrity articles.

- **Replace:** Call, text, or FaceTime an old friend you want to catch up with. Find out what is going on in their life, and share what is going on in yours.

- **Journal thought:** Why is it so easy to get pulled into juicy gossip? How does connecting with an old friend anchor you in what is important?

DAY 14

- **Repeal:** Instead of eating a meal in front of the television, make a connection plan.

- **Replace:** Plan a dinner out with your reboot partner(s). Plan to spend at least an hour together. Fill each other in on the details of how the reboot is impacting your view of friendship.

- **Journal thought:** Spend time talking to God about your reboot partner(s). Thank him for their friendship. Lift up their needs. Pray God's blessing over them.

Week 3 Scripture Focus

Read this portion of scripture every morning and night the third week to reset your thought patterns.

Philippians 4:4–9 (NKJV)

4 Rejoice in the Lord always. Again I will say, rejoice!

5 Let your gentleness be known to all men. The Lord is at hand.

6 Be anxious for nothing, but in everything by prayer and supplication, with thanksgiving, let your requests be made known to God;

7 and the peace of God, which surpasses all understanding, will guard your hearts and minds through Christ Jesus.

8 Finally, brethren, whatever things are true, whatever things are noble, whatever things are just, whatever things are pure, whatever things are lovely, whatever things are of good report, if there

is any virtue and if there is anything
praiseworthy—meditate on these things.

9 The things which you learned and received
and heard and saw in me, these do,
and the God of peace will be with you.

DAY 15

- **Repeal:** Instead of spending an hour scrolling through Reddit memes, get creative.

- **Replace:** Design your own encouraging pic using a quote or scripture, or create a funny meme using Pixlr or Canva. Text it to your friends and family; let them know how much joy they bring to your life.

- **Journal thought:** One of the greatest joys God gives is friendship. What are three ways you can connect better and be more of an encouragement to your friends?

DAY 16

- **Repeal:** Instead of posting more Instagram pictures or Facebook posts today, scroll through with a different idea in mind.

- **Replace:** Look through your last two weeks of photos, and notice all the amazing things and people that God has placed in your life.

- **Journal thought:** Using your feed as inspiration, list 10 things that you are grateful for. Spend time thanking God for his gifts and the people he has placed in your life.

DAY 17

- **Repeal:** Lose the negative and sarcastic comments that pop into your head when you see people's posts.

- **Replace:** Post 10 uplifting comments (not likes) on your friends' and family's posts today.

- **Journal thought:** What is your role in bringing positivity and joy into the lives of those around you? How do you reflect God's love with your words?

DAY 18

- **Repeal:** Take a break from YouTube and streaming entertainment videos.

- **Replace:** When you want to watch a video, find a sermon or an encouraging talk to watch. Share your thoughts or what you learned with your reboot partner.

- **Journal thought:** How does what you put in your mind affect your outlook on life? Are your thoughts and emotions impacted by what you watch?

DAY 19

- **Repeal:** Take a look at how much money you spend each month on streaming subscriptions. Determine if each outlet is actually benefiting your mental and emotional well-being.

- **Replace:** Match what you spend, and send that amount to a reputable relief organization like Convoy of Hope, World Vision, or Compassion International.

- **Journal thought:** How does loving God and loving others shape how you live your life?

DAY 20

- **Repeal:** Do a quick mental check. How is your outlook on life? If you have noticed that a certain social media impacts you in a negative way, delete that app.

- **Replace:** Read Philippians 4:8. Focus on the types of things you should be thinking about—things that are true, noble, right, pure, lovely, admirable, and excellent. Share these with your partner. Research shows that the brain releases serotonin and dopamine when you think about positive things like these, which are light-years more satisfying than shallow "likes" and thumb-ups.

- **Journal thought:** Record a different truth in your journal for each of the thought types (truc, noble, right, pure, lovely, admirable, excellent) in Philippians 4:8. Recognize how thinking these true, positive thoughts changes how you feel—God's happy prescription for your brain.

DAY 21

- **Repeal:** Lose the negativity for good.

- **Replace:** Celebrate with your reboot partner. Share the things you have learned over the past three weeks. Make a plan about how you want to continue to support each other and what actions you want to keep in place for the future.

- **Journal thought:** Think about what you are thinking about. How has the reboot changed the way you think about God and others?

Celebrate Your New Freedom

You may not feel like God's masterpiece right now. Maybe you are more like me and feel like a Picasso. But we are works in progress. Know that God promises to complete the good work he is doing in you, as you love him and love others! He longs for you to have freedom and experience real love.

Give yourself a high five for completing the commitment to the reboot. Start enjoying the well-deserved new freedom you are experiencing as you connect with God and others in true, authentic relationship.

Acknowledgments

Writing a book is very much a journey—and this journey was five years in the making. Along the way, God has worked through numerous people in my life to help create what you've just read. I could not finish this journey without acknowledging and giving thanks to the following friends and family members who inspired and encouraged me along the way.

Of course, I want to start with those who endured countless hours of conversations, trial ideas, sit-down reads, and first, second, third, and even 15th edits. That would be my wife, Michelle, and our two kids, Nate and Juliana. Thanks for your patience and input!

Many thanks to the Summit elders and leadership, for praying for and struggling through this process with me and for your ongoing support and encouragement. I am also grateful for the Summit family worldwide for striving to be real and authentic followers of Jesus Christ each and every day! You have big faith and even bigger hearts—you are the ones who keep me going and make the journey a joy!

You can't write a book like this without doing a lot of research. A big thank-you goes to the research team for helping me do what

I could not do alone, and especially to Joann Webster, for her invaluable expertise and insight, which transformed the contents of this book.

Thanks to everyone who set out to hurt and criticize me. Your posts, words, actions, and even trolling were meant for evil, but God turned them into something great as only he can do. See Romans 8:28 for the strength and inspiration on being a light in this dark world and for a far better way to live.

Finally, I'd like to thank you. Yes, *you*. Thank you for reading about how to take the modern-day kryptonite and learning how to leverage it for good! I pray this book will bless you and help you to live the life God has planned for you.

Notes

Read First

1. Huie, Jonathan Lockwood. "Fair Quotes and Sayings." https://www.jonathanlockwoodhuie.com/quotes/fair/.

Chapter 1

1. Kunst, Alexander. 2019. "Important Aspects in Life in the U.S. 2018." Statista. https://www.statista.com/forecasts/805855/most-important-values-in-life-in-the-us.

2. Bankmycell. 2020. "1 Billion More Phones Than People in the World!" Bankmycell. https://www.bankmycell.com/blog/how-many-phones-are-in-the-world.

3. Resnick, Brian. 2019. "22 Percent of Millennials Say They Have 'No Friends.'" Vox. https://www.vox.com/science-and-health/2019/8/1/20750047/millennials-poll-loncliness.

4. O'Donnell, Jayne, and Shari Rudavsky. 2018. "Young Americans Are the Loneliest, Surprising Cigna Study Shows." *USA Today.* https://www.usatoday.com/story/news/politics/2018/05/01/loneliness-poor-health-reported-far-more-among-young-people-than-even-those-over-72/559961002/.

5. Abbott, Brianna. 2019. "Youth Suicide Rate Increased 56% in Decade, CDC Says." *WSJ.* https://www.wsj.com/articles/youth-suicide-rate-rises-56-in-decade-cdc-says-11571284861.

6. Andros, Dan. 2019. "'I'm Watching This Over and Over Again': Jarrid Wilson's Wife Posts Gut-Wrenching Video Taken Just Hours Before His Death." *CBN News.* https://www1.cbn.com/cbnnews/2019/september/lsquo-i-rsquo-m-watching-this-over-and-over-again-rsquo-jarrid-wilson-rsquo-s-wife-posts-gut-wrenching-video-taken-just-hours-before-his-death.

7. Ratner, Paul. 2016. "Your Lifetime by the Numbers." Big Think. https://bigthink.com/paul-ratner/how-many-days-of-your-life-do-you-have-sex-your-lifetime-by-the-numbers.

8. McSweeney, Kelly. 2019. "This Is Your Brain on Instagram: Effects of Social Media on the Brain." Now: Powered by Northrop Grumman. https://now.northropgrumman.com/this-is-your-brain-on-instagram-effects-of-social-media-on-the-brain.

9. Hillard, Jena. 2019. "Social Media Addiction." Addiction Center. https://www.addictioncenter.com/drugs/social-media-addiction/.

10. McSweeney, Kelly. 2019. "This Is Your Brain on Instagram: Effects of Social Media on the Brain." Now: Powered by Northrop Grumman. https://now.northropgrumman.com/this-is-your-brain-on-instagram-effects-of-social-media-on-the-brain.

11. Merriam-Webster Online Dictionary. s.v. "like." Accessed April 29, 2020. https://www.merriam-webster.com/dictionary/like.

12. Yurieff, Kaya. 2018. "Snapchat Stock Loses $1.3 Billion after Kylie Jenner Tweet." *CNNmoney.* https://money.cnn.com/2018/02/22/technology/snapchat-update-kylie-jenner/index.html.

13. Chiu, Melody. 2020. "Taylor Swift and Kanye West's 'Famous' Phone Call Video Leaks Online — Read the Transcript." *People.* https://people.com/music/taylor-swift-kanye-west-famous-phone-call-leaks/.

14. IZEA. 2020. "Here Are the Highest Earning Instagrammers of 2020." IZEA. https://izea.com/2020/03/12/highest-earning-instagrammers/.

15. Steinbuch, Yaron. 2020. "Baby Yoda Is Trending Higher Than Most 2020 Democratic Hopefuls." *New York Post.* https://nypost.com/2019/11/29/baby-yoda-is-trending-higher-than-most-2020-democratic-hopefuls/.

16. CNN. 2013. "A Timeline of Anthony Weiner's Saga." *CNN.* https://www.cnn.com/2013/07/24/politics/weiner-timeline/index.html.

17. Sacks, Ethan. 2012. "Merriam-Webster's Collegiate Dictionary Adds

Sexting, f-Bombs, Man Cave and Other Words." *New York Daily News.*
https://www.nydailynews.com/news/national/merriam-webster-collegiate-
dictionary-adds-new-words-modern-world-article-1.1135696.

18. Malherbe, Petrus. 2015. "10 Really Weird Phobias That
Actually Exist." *News24.* https://www.news24.com/You/
Archive/10-really-weird-phobias-that-actually-exist-20170728.

19. Elmore, Tim. 2014. "Nomophobia: A Rising Trend in Students."
Psychology Today. https://www.psychologytoday.com/us/blog/
artificial-maturity/201409/nomophobia-rising-trend-in-students.

20. The Walt Disney Company. 2019. "Marvel Studios' 'Avengers: Endgame'
Makes History with $1.2 Billion Global Debut." The Walt Disney
Company. https://www.thewaltdisneycompany.com/marvel-studios-
avengers-endgame-makes-history-with-1-2-billion-global-debut/.

21. Cook, Sam. 2020. "Cyberbullying Statistics and Facts for 2020."
Comparitech. https://www.comparitech.com/internet-providers/
cyberbullying-statistics/.

22. Gayle, Latoya. 2019. "Kate Middleton Fan Has Copied 150 of the Duchess
of Cambridge's Outfits." *Daily Mail Online.* https://www.dailymail.co.uk/
femail/article-7127663/Mother-one-reveals-shes-copied-150-Duchess-
Cambridges-outfits.html.

23. News24. 2014. "Woman Has 36th Plastic Surgery Operation."
News24. https://www.news24.com/Drum/Archive/
woman-has-36th-plastic-surgery-operation-20170728.

24. Mizrahi, Gabriel. 2014. "Could Your FOMO Kill You?" *HuffPost.* https://
www.huffpost.com/entry/fomo_b_5130364.

25. Lickerman, Alex. 2010. "The Effect of Technology on Relationships."
Psychology Today. https://www.psychologytoday.com/us/blog/
happiness-in-world/201006/the-effect-technology-relationships.

26. Fuller, J. Ryan. "Social Media Use and Self-Esteem." New York Behavioral
Health. Accessed April 30, 2020. https://newyorkbehavioralhealth.com/
social-media-use-and-self-esteem.

27. Camp, Cassidy. 2017. "Social Media Is Making Us Invisible."
Uloop. https://www.uloop.com/news/view.php/239628/
Social-Media-is-Making-Us-Invisible.

28. Camp, Cassidy. 2017. "Social Media Is Making Us Invisible." Uloop. https://www.uloop.com/news/view.php/239628/ Social-Media-is-Making-Us-Invisible.

29. Meisenzahl, Mary. 2019. "Here's What Your Instagram Posts Will Look like without 'Likes'." *Business Insider.* https://www.businessinsider.com/ instagram-removing-likes-what-it-will-look-like-2019-11.

Chapter 2

1. Shamsian, Jacob, and Kelly McLaughlin. 2020. "Here's the Full List of People Charged in the College Admissions Cheating Scandal, and Who Has Pleaded Guilty so Far." Insider. https://www.insider.com/ college-admissions-cheating-scandal-full-list-people-charged-2019-3.

2. Kingslake, Rudolf, and Brian J. Thompson. 2020. "Optics." *Encyclopædia Britannica.* https://www.britannica.com/science/optics.

3. Bairstow, Jeff. 2010. "How Did Optics Become a Buzzword for PR." Laser Focus World. https://www.laserfocusworld.com/home/article/16568489/ how-did-optics-become-a-buzzword-for-pr.

4. History.com. 2009. "Galileo Is Convicted of Heresy." History.com. https:// www.history.com/this-day-in-history/galileo-is-convicted-of-heresy.

5. Florida State University. 2015. "Sir Isaac Newton. Molecular Expressions: Science, Optics and You." Florida State University. https://micro.magnet. fsu.edu/optics/timeline/people/newton.html.

6. Encyclopædia Britannica. 2020. "Hubble Space Telescope." *Encyclopædia Britannica.* https://www.britannica.com/topic/Hubble-Space-Telescope.

7. Pilkington, Ed. 2013. "Justine Sacco, PR Executive, Fired over Racist Tweet, 'Ashamed.'" *The Guardian.* https://www.theguardian.com/ world/2013/dec/22/pr-exec-fired-racist-tweet-aids-africa-apology.

8. Vingiano, Ali. 2019. "This Is How a Woman's Offensive Tweet Became the World's Top Story." *BuzzFeed News.* https://www.buzzfeednews.com/article/alisonvingiano/ this-is-how-a-womans-offensive-tweet-became-the-worlds-top-s.

9. Clement, J. 2019. "YouTube: Annual Beauty Content Views 2018." Statista. https://www.statista.com/statistics/294655/ youtube-monthly-beauty-content-views/.

10. Friedman, Megan. 2017. "TV Anchor Wears the Same Suit for a Year to Make a Point About Sexism." *ELLE*. https://www.elle.com/culture/movies-tv/news/a19279/tv-anchor-wears-same-suit/.

Chapter 3

1. Hagen-Miller, Linda. 2018. "Do You Know Somebody Who Suffers from Selfitis?" Heathline. https://www.healthline.com/health-news/do-you-know-somebody-who-suffers-from-selfitis#1.

2. Griffiths, Mark. 2019. "The Psychology of the Selfie." *Psychology Today*. https://www.psychologytoday.com/us/blog/in-excess/201905/the-psychology-the-selfie.

3. Eveleth, Rose. 2015. "How Many Photographs of You Are Out There in the World?" *The Atlantic*. https://www.theatlantic.com/technology/archive/2015/11/how-many-photographs-of-you-are-out-there-in-the-world/413389/.

4. Merriam-Webster Online Dictionary. s.v. "narcissism." Accessed April 30, 2020. https://www.merriam-webster.com/dictionary/narcissism.

5. Bible Gateway. "History of Israel—Encyclopedia of the Bible." Bible Gateway. Accessed April 30, 2020. https://www.biblegateway.com/resources/encyclopedia-of-the-bible/History-Israel.

6. Bible Gateway. "Period of Judges—Encyclopedia of the Bible." Bible Gateway. Accessed April 30, 2020. https://www.biblegateway.com/resources/encyclopedia-of-the-bible/Period-Judges.

7. Bible Gateway. "Saul—Encyclopedia of the Bible." Bible Gateway. Accessed April 30, 2020. https://www.biblegateway.com/resources/encyclopedia-of-the-bible/Saul.

8. 1 Samuel 8:1–22; 10:1–24; 11:1–15; 13:8–14; 14:1–15

9. 1 Samuel 9:2

10. 1 Samuel 16:14

11. Stites, Adam. 2017. "Here's a List of Every Major NFL Record Tom Brady Holds and the Ones He Can Still Break." SBNation.com. https://www.sbnation.com/2017/10/15/16464558/tom-brady-nfl-record-list-most-touchdowns-yards.

12. Gaines, Cork. 2019. "Tom Brady Was the Biggest Steal in NFL Draft History, but There Was More to It than Just Luck." *Business Insider.* https://www.businessinsider.com/patriots-draft-tom-brady-2017-1.

13. 1 Samuel 16:7

14. 1 Samuel 16:1–14

15. Bible Gateway. "David—Encyclopedia of the Bible." Bible Gateway. Accessed April 30, 2020. https://www.biblegateway.com/resources/encyclopedia-of-the-bible/David.

16. Bair, Andrew. 2013. "Dismemberment Abortions: The Baby's Head Is Crushed and Extracted in Pieces." Life News. https://www.lifenews.com/2015/02/05/dismemberment-abortions-the-babys-head-is-crushed-and-extracted-in-pieces/.

17. Funke, Daniel. 2020. "How the Black Lives Matter Global Network Is Set Up." Politifact. https://www.politifact.com/factchecks/2020/jun/17/candace-owens/how-black-lives-matter-global-network-set/.

18. Kern, Soeren. 2020. "Black Lives Matter: 'We Are Trained Marxists' – Part 1." Gatestone Institute. https://www.gatestoneinstitute.org/16181/black-lives-matter.

19. Johnson, Ben. 2020. "Explainer: What Does Black Lives Matter Believe?" Acton. https://www.acton.org/publications/transatlantic/2020/06/18/explainer-what-does-black-lives-matter-believe.

20. Blackman, Walt. 2020. "Abortion: The Overlooked Tragedy for Black Americans." *Arizona Capitol Times.* https://azcapitoltimes.com/news/2020/02/25/abortion-the-overlooked-tragedy-for-black-americans/.

Chapter 4

1. Crabtree, Erin. 2019. "The Bachelor: Why Colton (Finally!) Jumped the Fence." *Us Weekly.* https://www.usmagazine.com/entertainment/news/the-bachelor-why-colton-jumped-the-fence/.

2. Longeretta, Emily. 2020. "Colton Underwood and Cassie Randolph's Relationship Timeline." *Us Weekly.* https://www.usmagazine.com/celebrity-news/pictures/colton-underwood-cassie-randolphs-relationship-timeline/march-2020-11/.

3. Lin, Melissa. 2018. "Online Dating Industry: The Business of Love." Toptal Finance Blog. https://www.toptal.com/finance/business-model-consultants/online-dating-industry.

4. Hoff, Victoria Dawson. 2017. "I Joined a Beard-Themed Dating Site." *ELLE*. https://www.elle.com/life-love/sex-relationships/advice/a14878/bristlr-beard-dating/.

5. Shocket, Ryan. 2019. "21 Hilarious Dating App Fails from This Year." *BuzzFeed*. https://www.buzzfeed.com/ryanschocket2/hilarious-tinder-messages-people-actually-recei-1.

6. Fetters, Ashley. 2020. "The Five Years That Changed Dating." *The Atlantic*. https://www.theatlantic.com/family/archive/2018/12/tinder-changed-dating/578698/.

7. Lewis, C. S., and Zach Kincaid. 2020. "Four Types of Love." CSLewis.com. https://www.cslewis.com/four-types-of-love/.

8. Sharma, Ananta. 2015. "9 Real-Life Friendship Stories from Around the Globe That Will Move Your Heart." Storypick. https://www.storypick.com/real-moving-friendship-stories/.

9. Pelletiere, Nicole. 2019. "Single Dad Who Fostered 30 Kids Adopts 5 Siblings under 5 Years Old." *Good Morning America*. https://www.goodmorningamerica.com/family/story/single-dad-fostered-30-kids-adopts-siblings-years-66499941.

10. Tallerico, Brian. 2016. "La La Land Movie Review & Film Summary." Roger Ebert. https://www.rogerebert.com/reviews/la-la-land-2016.

11. Shakespeare Birthplace Trust. "Romeo and Juliet." Shakespeare Birthplace Trust. Accessed April 30, 2020. https://www.shakespeare.org.uk/explore-shakespeare/shakespedia/shakespeares-plays/romeo-and-juliet/.

12. Chan, Francis, and Danae Yankoski. 2013. *Crazy Love: Overwhelmed by a Relentless God*. Colorado Springs, CO: David C. Cook.

13. Mark 12:30–31

14. Christianity.com. 2010. "Jim Elliot: Story and Legacy." Christianity.com. https://www.christianity.com/church/church-history/timeline/1-300/jim-elliot-no-fool-11634862.html.

15. Mission Aviation Fellowship. "Life Magazine—The Martyrs' Story." Mission Aviation Fellowship. Accessed April 30, 2020. https://www.maf-uk.org/story/life-magazine-the-martyrs-story.

16. Peña, Madeline. 2020. "Jim and Elisabeth Elliot: Devotion to the Unreached." BGU's College of Missions. https://bethanygu.edu/blog/ stories/jim-and-elisabeth-elliot/#met.

17. Psalm 136

Chapter 5

1. Goldberg, Matt. 2019. "Marvel Studios at the Box Office: How Much Has Each Film Made?" Collider. https://collider.com/ marvel-movies-box-office/#worldwide-totals-ranked.

2. Catsoulis, Jeannette. 2015. "Review: In 'Batkid Begins,' a Boy's Simple Wish Whips Up Frenzied Adulation." *The New York Times*. https://www. nytimes.com/2015/06/26/movies/review-in-batkid-begins-a-boys-simple-wish-whips-up-frenzied-adulation.html.

3. Mandell, Andrea. 2015. "5 Things You Never Knew about 'Batkid.'" *USA Today*. https://www.usatoday.com/story/life/movies/2015/06/24/ batkid-begins-five-things-you-dont-know/29141327/.

4. Nicholson, Amy. 2019. "You Thought You Were a Good Person for Getting Weepy Over the Batkid Video. You Were Wrong." *LA Weekly*. https://www. laweekly.com/you-thought-you-were-a-good-person-for-getting-weepy-over-the-batkid-video-you-were-wrong/.

5. Comic-Cons.xyz. 2020. "Biggest Comic Conventions in US by Attendance." Comic-Cons.xyz. http://comic-cons.xyz/ biggest-comic-cons-us/.

6. FanCons.com. "Upcoming Worldwide Comic Convention Schedule." FanCons.com. Accessed April 30, 2020. https://fancons.com/events/ schedule.php?type=comic.

7. Free, Erin. 2016. "The Age of Heroes: Why Are Superhero Movies So Popular?" FilmInk. https://www.filmink.com.au/ the-age-of-heroes-why-are-superhero-movies-so-popular/.

8. Chokshi, Niraj. 2019. "Americans Are Among the Most Stressed People in the World, Poll Finds." *The New York Times*. https://www.nytimes. com/2019/04/25/us/americans-stressful.html.

9. New York Post. 2017. "Americans Spend 4 Years of Their Lives 'Escaping Reality.'" *New York Post*. https://nypost.com/2017/07/03/ americans-spend-4-years-of-their-lives-escaping-reality/.

10. MIDiA Research. 2019. "Consumers Spend 4.5 Hours per Day on Digital Entertainment." MIDiA Research. https://www.midiaresearch.com/blog/consumers-spend-4-5-hours-per-day-on-digital-entertainment/.

11. Bible Gateway. "David—Encyclopedia of the Bible." Bible Gateway. Accessed April 30, 2020. https://www.biblegateway.com/resources/encyclopedia-of-the-bible/David.

12. 1 Samuel 17:1–51

13. Bible Gateway. "Saul—Encyclopedia of the Bible." Bible Gateway. Accessed April 30, 2020. https://www.biblegateway.com/resources/encyclopedia-of-the-bible/Saul.

14. Exodus 14:21

15. Esther 7:3–8

16. Daniel 3:16–18

17. 1 Samuel 18:6–7

18. Harvey-Jenner, Catriona. 2017. "The Psychology of a Like: How Social Media Is Really Affecting Your Brain." *Cosmopolitan.* https://www.cosmopolitan.com/uk/reports/a9931660/psychology-social-media-likes-mental-health-issues/.

19. Dictionary.com. 2020. s.v. "Cancel Culture." Dictionary.com. https://www.dictionary.com/e/pop-culture/cancel-culture/.

20. Fink, Sheri. 2020. "Worst-Case Estimates for U.S. Coronavirus Deaths." *The New York Times.* https://www.nytimes.com/2020/03/13/us/coronavirus-deaths-estimate.html.

Chapter 6

1. Winchell, Walter. 1954. "Hottest Scandal in Town." *The Washington Post.* https://quoteinvestigator.com/2019/05/07/friend-walk/#note-435364-7.

2. Diesel, Vin, James Gunn, Nicole Perlman, Dan Abnett, Andy Lanning. 2014. *Guardians of the Galaxy.* DVD. Directed by James Gunn. New York: Marvel.

3. Dumas, Alexandre, and William Robson. 1922. *The Three Musketeers.* London: George Rutledge and Sons, ltd.

4. Evans, Chris, Stephen McFeely, and Christopher Markus. 2014. *Captain America: The Winter Soldier*. DVD. Directed by Anthony Russo and Joe Russo. New York: Marvel.

5. Irvin, Doyle. 2017. "'You'll Be My Arms. I'll Be Your Eyes': A Story of Two Disabled Men Who've Planted More Than 10,000 Trees." American Forests. https://www.americanforests.org/blog/youll-arms-ill-eyes-story-two-disabled-men-whove-planted-10000-trees/.

6. Great Big Story. 2016. "The Friends Who Planted 10,000 Trees." YouTube video. https://www.youtube.com/watch?v=C2cqQA_zsKY.

7. Degges-White, Suzanne. 2015. "The 13 Essential Traits of Good Friends." *Psychology Today*. https://www.psychologytoday.com/us/blog/lifetime-connections/201503/the-13-essential-traits-good-friends.

8. Mayo Clinic. 2019. "The Health Benefits of Good Friends." Mayo Clinic. https://www.mayoclinic.org/healthy-lifestyle/adult-health/in-depth/friendships/art-20044860.

9. 1 Samuel 18:1–4; 1 Sam 20:1–42

10. 1 Samuel 18:10–11; 1 Sam 19:1–10

11. 1 Samuel 20:32

12. Duke Health. 2019. "Donated Kidney Saves Best Friend's Life." Duke Health. https://www.dukehealth.org/blog/donated-kidney-saves-best-friends-life.

13. Scott, Jess C. 2011. *The Other Side of Life*. CreateSpace.

14. Sharma, Ananta. 2015. "9 Real-Life Friendship Stories from Around the Globe That Will Move Your Heart." Storypick. https://www.storypick.com/real-moving-friendship-stories/.

15. 2 Samuel 9:1

16. 2 Samuel 4:4; 2 Sam 9:1–12

Chapter 7

1. The Globe and Mail. 2007. "Superman's Kryptonite Confirmed in Canada." *The Globe and Mail*. https://www.theglobeandmail.com/technology/science/supermans-kryptonite-confirmed-in-canada/article683958/.

2. Christensen, Bill. 2008. "Real Mineral Nearly Identical to Superman's Kryptonite." LiveScience. https://www.livescience.com/1467-real-mineral-identical-superman-kryptonite.html.

3. Burke, Minyvonne. 2018. "Two California Nuns Accused of Embezzling Half a Million from School for Trips and Gambling." NBCNews.com. https://www.nbcnews.com/news/us-news/two-california-nuns-accused-embezzling-half-million-school-trips-gambling-n946056.

4. StateParks.com. "Stone Mountain State Park." StateParks.com. Accessed May 1, 2020. https://www.stateparks.com/stone_mountain_state_park_in_north_carolina.html.

5. Hubbard, Jule. 2012. "Teen Dies in Fall at Stone Mountain." *Journalpatriot*. https://www.journalpatriot.com/news/teen-dies-in-fall-at-stone-mountain/article_3474a860-066e-11e2-a3ad-0019bb30f31a.html.

6. 2 Samuel 11:1–27

7. 2 Samuel 23:8, 39

8. 2 Samuel 12:1–24

9. Psalm 119:11

Chapter 8

1. Segal, Robert. 2020. "Joseph Campbell." *Encyclopædia Britannica*. https://www.britannica.com/biography/Joseph-Campbell-American-author.

2. Bronzite, Dan. "The Hero's Journey—Mythic Structure of Joseph Campbell's Monomyth." Movie Outline—Screenwriting Software. Accessed May 1, 2020. http://www.movieoutline.com/articles/the-hero-journey-mythic-structure-of-joseph-campbell-monomyth.html.

3. Fisher, Carrie and George Lucas. 1977. *Star Wars*. DVD. Directed by George Lucas. Los Angeles: 20th Century Fox.

4. Coggan, Devan, and Tyler Aquilina. 2019. "Here's How Every 'Star Wars' Movie Did at the Box Office." EW.com. https://ew.com/movies/star-wars-movies-box-office-comparison/.

5. Reference for Business. "Fred Smith 1944–." Reference for Business. Accessed May 1, 2020. https://www.referenceforbusiness.com/biography/S-Z/Smith-Fred-1944.html.

6. 1 Samuel 24:1–22

7. 1 Samuel 31:1–13; 2 Samuel 1:1–27

8. Biography.com. 2019. "David Livingstone." Biography.com. https://www. biography.com/explorer/david-livingstone.

9. Encyclopædia Britannica. 2020. "Eric Liddell." *Encyclopædia Britannica.* https://www.britannica.com/biography/Eric-Liddell.

10. Christianity Today. 2019. "Hudson Taylor." *Christianity Today.* https://www. christianitytoday.com/history/people/missionaries/hudson-taylor.html.

11. Leadership Resources. 2016. "The 15 Best James Hudson Taylor Quotes." Leadership Resources. https://www.leadershipresources.org/ the-15-best-james-hudson-taylor-quotes/.

Chapter 9

1. Meyers, Stephen. 2018. "Top 5 Beginner Fourteeners." *Coloradoan.* https://www.coloradoan.com/story/sports/outdoors/2014/06/27/ top-beginner-fourteeners/11474973/.

2. Grady, Mike. 2018. "Group Counted 334,000 People Hiking on Colorado's 14ers in 2017." KUSA.com. https://www.9news.com/article/ news/local/next/group-counted-334000-people-hiking-on-colorados- 14ers-in-2017/73-581856945.

3. Achs, Jordan. 2015. "Andrew Hamilton Shatters Colorado 14ers Speed Record." *Climbing Magazine.* https://www.climbing.com/news/ andrew-hamilton-shatters-colorado-14ers-speed-record/.

4. Jane. 2019. "The Dreaded Marathon DNF and How to Prevail." Ready.Set.Marathon. https://readysetmarathon.com/ the-dreaded-marathon-dnf-and-how-to-prevail/.

5. Psalm 23:4

6. 1 Samuel 27:1–12

7. Ziglar, Zig. 2017. "We All Need a Daily Check-Up." Ziglar Inc. https:// www.ziglar.com/quotes/we-all-need-a-daily-check-up-from/.

8. 1 Samuel 30:1–31

9. 2 Samuel 15:1–37

10. James 1:2–5

Chapter 10

1. Rubenstein, Steve. 2012. "BAKERSFIELD / Beloved Missionary Killed in Drive-by Shooting in Iraq." *SFGate*. https://www.sfgate.com/bayarea/article/BAKERSFIELD-Beloved-missionary-killed-in-2808206.php.

2. 2 Samuel 7:14–16

3. John 1:46

4. John 4:1–42

5. McFadden, Robert D. 2014. "Hiroo Onoda, Soldier Who Hid in Jungle for Decades, Dies at 91." *The New York Times*. https://www.nytimes.com/2014/01/18/world/asia/hiroo-onoda-imperial-japanese-army-officer-dies-at-91.html.

6. Matthew 26:36–75

7. Matthew 27:11–56

8. John 3:16

9. Luke 23:34

About the Author

Photography by Michael Allen Creative

Rob's journey as a pastor began one night, alone, on a 40-acre island in the heart of the Adirondack Mountains. Like Jacob in the Old Testament, he was wrestling with God about which way to go with his life. Before the night was over, God won, and the 16-year-old knew he would never be the same!

After high school, Rob returned to that island (Word of Life Island) and attended Word of Life Bible Institute for one year of deep instruction. Then, he attended Dallas Theological Seminary, where he received his ThM (Master of Theology degree) and completed a three-year stint as the North Dallas area director for Young Life. Young Life gave him the opportunity to apply all that he was learning with young people who were unchurched and, in some cases, completely unaware of Jesus Christ and his rescue mission for their souls over 2,000 years ago.

After seminary, Rob moved to Charlotte, North Carolina, and met his wife and ministry partner, Michelle. Together, they have directly planted three churches and assisted in planting seven others. A pastor for nearly 25 years and a mentor and friend to some of today's best-known pastors and Christian leaders, he continues to minister as the lead pastor at The Summit Church in Centennial, Colorado. His vision has long been to reach those far from God, raise them up in Christ, and release them into the community to fulfill the Great Commission and Great Commandment.

More information about Rob, his ministry, booking him for speaking opportunities, and connecting with him in general can be found on robsingleton.com.